STUDIES IN ART

Volume I

MOJMÍR S. FRINTA

THE GENIUS
OF
ROBERT CAMPIN

1966

MOUTON & CO · THE HAGUE

PARIS

LIBRARY OF CONGRESS CATALOG CARD NUMBER: 65-24785

1000423420

Printed in The Netherlands by Mouton & Co., Printers, The Hague.

Preface

Few ensembles of painting which are decisive in determining the course of European painting are as notorious a subject of ardent investigation—and, occasionally, heated controversy—as the Flemish masterpieces of the first half of the fifteenth century grouped around the names of Roger van der Weyden and Master of Flémalle, tentatively identified as Robert Campin. Since the identification by Wilhelm Bode in 1887 and Hugo von Tschudi in 1898 of a group of paintings united by the same style and spirit as works of a painter other than Roger, this thesis has been accepted by more and more researchers. The nucleus of the oeuvre was formed by the large panels in the Städelsches Kunstinstitut in Frankfurt and by the Annunciation triptych which was for a long time in the possession of the Merode family. The formers' alleged provenience from the Abbey (sic) Flémalle near Liège provided the namesake for their author, the Master of Flémalle.[1]

1   The history of the investigation is vast and involves the most prominent scholars in the field. A very brief summary may be offered here. The opponents of the "dualistic" thesis adhered to the "unitarian" belief by maintaining that these paintings represent the early phase of van der Weyden's art. On the other hand, the majority considered (and consider) them creations of a teacher of Roger, and Robert Campin, whom the records show to have been a painter in Tournai between 1406 and 1444, was the most logical choice. Campin was born somewhere between 1375 and 1378, became a citizen of Tournai in 1410 and died there on April 26, 1444. About his origin nothing is known and to the hypothesis that he was from Valenciennes (families of the name Campin are

Not a single painting may be safely attributed to Campin on grounds of historical record as not one bears his signature nor a date (with the exception of one, the validity of which I shall discuss later). The grouping was done on the basis of stylistic analysis from which an evolution of his art was supposedly established. The number of attributions vary with various scholars but it must be acknowledged that the core of the attributions represents a truly remarkable, homogeneous and highly personal style.

The oeuvre of Roger van der Weyden seems to rest on somewhat firmer ground, but after rigorous scrutiny of all evidence we are left with the realization that the situation is not much better here. The documented monumental

---

documented there) may be juxtaposed another perhaps more interesting, that he came from the northern part of Brabant called De Kempen (La Campine).

The previously (1902) proposed identification by Hulin de Loo with another Tournai painter and fellow student of Roger, Jacques Daret, was abandoned by Hulin in favor of Campin when he found in 1909 the panels of the Arras retable which could be shown by the records to be Daret's work. The "unitarians" refused to accept the interpretation of the somewhat confusing documents which identified a pupil of Campin, Rogelet de la Pasture (apprenticed in 1427-32) as Roger van der Weyden. The fact elicited from documents that Roger was called "maistre" and honored by the town of Tournai at the time of his visit even before becoming an apprentice is certainly strange. Baffling is also the recurring reference in Italian, almost contemporary, sources to the famous painter Roger of Bruges. This led C. Hasse (*Roger van Brügge, der Meister von Flémalle*, Strassburg, 1904) to assume that there existed at the same time two prominent painters by the name of Roger.

The most ardent of the attackers in the late twenties was Emile Renders, who, using sets of morphological comparisons, tried to prove that there was only one author for both groups of paintings. Louis Beyaert-Carlier (1937), and before him, Paul Jamot (1928) took a similar line. This position was also adopted by J. Lavalleye (1933). Max J. Friedländer abandoned his original conviction, voiced in the second volume of his history of old Netherlands painting, that two artists were involved and changed his mind in his later volumes after the discovery in 1931 of the Abegg triptych from Turin. Theodor Musper has recently become a partisan of the movement for the abolition of the existence of the Master of Flémalle (1948). Yet the majority of present-day scholars object to the telescoping of Flémalle-Campin and van der Weyden. All the bibliography is to be found in Erwin Panofsky, *Early Netherlandish Painting*. Cambridge, Massachusetts, 1953.

There is no doubt in my mind about the separate existence of the two painters. My belief grew even stronger after my investigation of Campin's paintings when one of the major obstacles to the understanding of their respective artistic profiles had been removed, as I have elaborated in the latter part of my study. I prefer to use the name of Campin to the "Master of Flémalle", as the latter lacks factual accuracy and in the absence of evidence to the contrary this identification may be considered both reasonable and practical.

I am concerned less with the identification of the author of this tightly-knit group of paintings with some historical personality, Robert Campin or any other for that matter: my chief aim is to find out by stylistico-technical analysis which paintings are really by one single hand, and appreciate his specific capacity as an artist.

paintings in Brussels City Hall are lost and even the cornerstones of his production reveal themselves to be resting on foundations which are not as firm as we would have liked to assume, as they are identified with Roger only by later testimonies.

In the present study I shall attempt to establish the essential features of Campin's art covering composition, organization of masses, spatial representation, chromatic vision, morphological peculiarities, brushwork and other technical procedures. On the basis of those findings I shall endeavor to characterize his style and his artistic personality. My judgements and conclusions are based on exhaustive observation of the painted surface of the panels, combined with the interpretation of X-ray and infra-red photographs whenever available.[2] For this task I am conditioned by the background of an art historian, restorer and painter, a hybrid combination, but not as disparate as that of Hans Sachs' *Schuhmacher und Poeta dazu.*

It is indeed a formidable task to unravel the truth from the maze of inevitably subjective judgments and hypotheses often presented *bona fide* as facts when one is not equipped with sound external evidence. The problem calls for a scientific examination of the paintings dissociated from the preconceived patterns of thinking formed only by secondary sources. Research based on these secondary sources has encountered some stylistic problems, some supposed borrowings and some baffling vacillating influences. It was therefore necessary for their solution to develop a series of involved hypotheses suggesting the existence of complex mutual influences between the two protagonists of the style, Roger van der Weyden and Robert Campin. These proposals were devised in an attempt to rationalize the inconsistencies and to bridge over or at least to attenuate the apparent inconsistencies and contradictions in the evolutions of these two painters as they were proposed to have occurred.

The basic problem here is to learn to discern the formal and expressive characteristics of the painter, his chromatic and compositional predilections

2   I am greatly obliged to a number of persons and institutions who gave me valuable help in one or more of the following ways: granting me the permission to study certain paintings, consulting the documentation, supplying me with photographs, information, advice. I would like to thank especially Dr. P. Coremans, Centre de Recherches Primitifs Flamands, Brussels; Mr. M. Davies, National Gallery, London; Dr. Eich, Staedelsches Kunstinstitut, Frankfort; Madame M. Hours, Services du Laboratoire du Musée du Louvre; Mr. Loewinson-Lessing, Gosudarstvennij Ermitaż, Leningrad; Mademoiselle L. Ninane, Musée Royal d'Art Ancien, Brussels; M. P. Quarré, Musée de Dijon; Count Antoine Seilern, London; Mademoiselle N. Verhaegen, Centre de Recherches Primitifs Flamands, Brussels; Kress Foundation, New York; The Metropolitan Museum of Art, New York. — Unfortunately, not all panels considered here were subject to a physico-chemical examination and several useful data are thus not available. I regret that I was unable to obtain the permission to publish some X-ray photographs.

and solutions: to pierce so to speak the *thalamus* of his creative imagination and to try to perceive the range and possibilities beyond which he seemed never to have ventured. The effort to identify oneself with the artist's world of ideas and forms, his capacity and limits, is possible only when one finds in oneself the sympathetic response to the particular type and mode of creation. This raises the problem confronting history of art which in its zeal to be a scientific dicipline occasionally appropriates pseudo-scientific attitudes to arrive at a solution. Yet the very subject defeats any more rigidly materialistic and synthesizing attitude. I do not propose to depend on intuition but more on intense observation, imaginative speculation, psychological interpretation—and last but not least—love and compassion toward the object of study *sine qua non.*

In my analysis I hope to show that the characteristic idioms of Campin's art, established from the study of the basic works, are not present in all works currently assigned to him and that these idioms stand out in a startingly clear way in a couple of masterpieces not previously associated with Campin. I shall endeavor to grasp the quintessence of Campin's uniqueness and bring together only that which emanates from a common spirit.[3]

Stylistic connoisseurship cannot exist without a profound knowledge of the technical aspects of the work of art. The study of brushwork, underdrawing and its relation to the painting, construction of paint layers and choice of pigments should be considered a means of penetrating the psychology and temperament of the artist. The study of chromatic characteristics plays an important role but the discussion of color is difficult—and it is perhaps even impossible to make it convincing—not only because the subtleties of the sensations registered by the eye cannot be adequately described in words but also because different eyes perceive colors differently. This may perhaps be the reason why the discussion of color is so rarely introduced into the analysis of a work apart from the fact that only a fraction of researchers are acutely sensitive to the subtle differentiation of color values and to the relationship of these to technical procedures (e.g. a mixture of specific pigments achieves a particular tone modulated often by the method of the application of the paint—in glazes, variated layers, rich or lean in painting medium, etc.). These few grasp the role of chromatic choices in the creative act. I believe that the

---

3   The pitfalls of this analytico-stylistic approach are many. Analogies based on compositional, typological, morphological and iconographical comparisons, though highly useful, cannot always be trusted. It is a known fact that pupils, followers, collaborators and competitors could copy a master's compositional devices, facial types and gestures in a most convincing way. It is necessary therefore to go beyond the outward appearance and to penetrate the spirit underlying the creation and to detect inimitable technical details, since, in the absence of an authentic élan common to all the related works, it is impossible to assign them to a single creator.

study of the *coloris* in correlation with other critical criteria may help to reveal the artistic personality and be useful especially for works believed to belong to one phase of the artist's production. Some chromatic characteristics such as the mixing of certain pigments to produce the shading of a flesh color are usually present in the artist's works from a certain period but may be subject to gradual supplementation. Predilections for certain colors and their instinctive matching to produce certain moods may change with the artist's progressing career, apart, of course, from the imposed conventions, iconographic requirements and occasional explicit wishes of a patron, which are, I believe, on the whole not very significant for the connoisseurship. Many of these semi-automatic or instinctive operations, together with the realization of such qualities as mellowness of harmony, its warmth or coolness, overharmonization or brutal and bold contrasting, may remain constant throughout the period of his maturity.[4]

4 Certain colors (hues, not necessarily pigments) seem to be in vogue in certain regions and schools at a certain time. Besides the practical reasons for their use (local availability, circumstances of supply), their occurrence may be due to the taste of some influential artist rather than to the expression of a mythical and abstract "regional character".

Contents

CHAPTER I

The Annunciation Triptych in New York

(Merode Altarpiece)

My investigation of Campin's technique and artistic personality was initiated by study of formal, technical and expressive means in the Annunciation triptych (Merode retable) when it emerged from seclusion. My interest was focussed on the relationship of the three panels of the triptych and specifically on that of the donor's panel to the other two. Remarks have been made about certain incongruities: some writers have wondered about the uneven perspective which is steeper in the center and right-hand panels and flatter in the left-hand one, the different scale of figures in the two parts and the different gamut of colors. No conclusions were drawn, however, because the work itself was so full of revolution and innovation.

Let us examine successively the peculiarities in the construction of space and perspective, the composition, the role of light and shade, the chromatic conception and painting technique. For the sake of conciseness, the central panel and the right-hand wing will be referred to as A, and B will denote the left-hand wing with the donors.

A. Immediately striking is the peculiar treatment of the masses, which are expressed most clearly in their basic forms to achieve an effect of utmost tangibility. The furrows of shade envelop the contours of forms as moats encircle fortresses and heighten the three-dimensional effect. Theodore Rousseau has very aptly emphasized the relief character of the paintings.[1] They are indeed constructed on the principle of a dish-like development of the relief

1 "The Merode Altarpiece", *The Metropolitan Museum of Art Bulletin,* December 1957, p. 124. The closest stylistic comparison of the two media is offered in a fragment

surface. The figures are almost on the projection plane, reaching up to the level of the rim of the dish, so to speak, with only small objects in front of them. Overlapping, which presents problems in the construction of the elevations and obscures the eloquency of forms, is instinctively avoided whenever possible.

The ups and downs of the shapes bulge and recede in a continuous rhythm as if a fabric has been thrown over the actual forms, which gets caught on the protruding parts, falls steeply into the hollows and again surges up to reach the next elevation. This is a comfortable and efficient solution which avoids all problems of the representation of the space enveloping the objects and does not deprive them of all support, as they grow out of the rear plane.

The solidity achieved by unalterably anchoring the juxtaposed forms into the composition is quite consistent with their apparent massiveness. This, in addition to the stocky dimensions of the furniture and the figures themselves, reveals the master's taste for order and tangibility.

B.   Here there is an apparent disregard for relief construction. The painter has composed the masses by superimposing various planes like the wings on the sides of the stage which lack the solidity of the third dimension. Departing completely from the structural principles of the dish-type of relief is the design of the door which extends forward out of the picture plane and past the figure of the donor. It would be more in keeping with the relief principle to represent the door as opening in the other direction, toward the rear plane. Furthermore, the kneeling figures, contrary to the relief conception, are removed from the extreme foreground in a more painterly manner. The rosebush is a wiry, lattice-like substance and the author of A would never have painted this bulkless form next to the light surface of the door but would rather have created there a broad contrasting shape of a spatially receding pocket of darkness. Unlike A, the painter here was not concerned with representing the massiveness of objects. The impression, in fact, tends in the opposite direction. The wall and the gatehouse are almost papery despite their suggested third dimension.

A.   The perspective, the suggested distances and the proportions have a definite consistency about them that creates an impression of verisimilitude. The deviations and inaccuracies are never shocking since they conform to the predetermined pattern of spatial representation.

A strong underlying striving toward the centrality of the two panels is created by their converging toward the emphasized focal point. Though each panel has its own vanishing point, the spatial unity of view is somehow not disturbed by these separate constructions. It would be quite incorrect to expect one

---

of a stela in Tournai. Paul Rolland, "Stèles funéraires tournaisiennes gothiques", *Revue belge d'archéologie et d'histoire de l'art*, XX, 1951, pp. 189-222, Figs. 5 and 6.

central vanishing point, as some writers have done.[2] That would result in a rigid and pedantically artificial construction. This supposed ignorance on the part of the painter is indeed much closer to a true and successive grasp of the twin spaces which are to be represented. To experience them simultaneously would be absurd, and one has to move sidewise from a fixed position somewhere in front of the main group to a new position corresponding to the space of the carpenter's shop. Perhaps the shop does not even adjoin, because we get a feeling from the view of clouds through the window in the living room that we are on the second floor.

The perspective of the central panel converges abruptly into one vanishing point centered between the Virgin and the angel, i.e. along the axis on which the spectator would logically stand when contemplating the scene. The horizon is quite high and runs above the middle of the window as can be expected in a full-front view. In the right-hand panel the horizon appears to be slightly lower and the perpendicular lines converge into a vanishing point of their own.

The benches and tables are exaggeratedly tilted upward in an archaic way to show more of their tops. This temporary shifting of the viewpoint is also usual in the above-mentioned type of relief construction. It may, moreover, in addition to being a facet of traditionalism, reflect the Master's sophisticated desire to represent a shift of focus when the eye moves from a distant vista to the observation of a detail in the foreground.

B. The leitmotif of the upward centripetal force in the composition of A is not apparent here except in the design of the right-hand foreground. On the other hand, the view through the gate into the street introduces a centrifugal note into the composition as it catches the spectator's attention and leads it sideways. The only centripetal element, i.e. the steps and the open door, is doubtless an ingenious device aiming at pictorial and thematic unity. This *tour de force,* however, is somewhat too intellectual an arrangement lacking the spontaneity of design that distinguishes the other panels. Moreover, the door does not correspond to the door opening partly visible at the edge of the central panel. It is as if the painter wanted at all costs to link the left-hand wing with the center piece by this original but too obvious trick when it became apparent that his own artistic temperament did not enable him to achieve a completely convincing unity in spirit.

The perspective and distances, while aspiring to be correct, are in reality just a conglomeration of unrelated elements. The contradiction between the suggested deeply receding courtyard and some of the proportions which correlate and diminish at a different and much slower pace is certainly disturbing (cf. the rosebush v. the standing man, the gatehouse v. the birds, the wide open door in the foreground v. the kneeling donor).

2   David Robb, *The Harper History of Painting* (New York, 1951), p. 173.

The sorest spot for an eye trained in geometry is the area around the gate in the enclosure wall. The open door and the standing man belong to a system with a short focal distance and a low horizon, whereas the masonry of the doorway is presented in a long-range perspective with a much higher horizon. The result is a fluctuation of horizon and focal distance.[3]

Unlike A, where the spatial transition is smooth and continuous, often using the device of eye-leading pieces of furniture, there is here practically no transition from one plane to another because of the *coulisses* arrangement.

The problem of including a large amount of background with the foreground, all crammed on to a narrow surface, is, of course, a much more ambitious task and a tricky one to solve.

A. The surface is enlivened by a swiftly changing pattern of light and dark areas which meet in strongly contrasting values. The light area sharply borders on a dark area and an abstract and dramatic tension is created. Yet the boldness does not lack grace. The movement of the surface might be compared to an artfully crumpled tinfoil which catches light on ridges and peaks. The drama in the details, such as the angled drapery, the blown-out flame and the animated leaves in the open book, is overruled by the pristinely cool and quiet surface of the walls. The warp of long and straight directional lines is sensitively counterbalanced by the suspended and interwoven curves and breaks which characterize smaller shapes. Several forms are aligned to establish a sensitively intervalled vertical network.[4] The forms join and compose themselves into larger units by the device of leading the outline of one form directly into another,[5] while elsewhere barely touching, and thus help to restore the plane of the picture that is threatened by the relief concept.

B. The pattern of light and dark shapes calls to mind a "collage" rather than the fully integrated ups and downs of the relief manner in A. The overlapping of shapes conveys less of an impression of a visual rhythm, since the

3 It is interesting to note that this seemingly advanced and sophisticated representation of perspective, betraying in a few instances a lack of understanding of its laws and an absence of the corrective faculty derived from direct observation, occurs in some works of Roger van der Weyden. Very similar deformation exists in the Annunciation in the Louvre on one of the foreshortened shutters and on the door jambs in the dexter wall. Similarly, the castle in the Visitation panel from the collection of Speck von Sternburg in Lützschena shows a bad perspective and somewhat lacks the illusion of the third dimension. Panofsky, *op.cit.*, Figs. 310 and 311. Gatehouses similar to that in the donor's wing occur in Roger's works, i.e. in the Lützschena panel and in the large Annunciation in the Metropolitan Museum of Art.

4 The Virgin's head and the shutters, the candlestick and the mullion of the window, the leg of the table and the towel, the axis of the jug and the edge of the window-jamb, etc.

5 Already observed by Otto Pächt, "Gestaltungprinzipien der westlichen Malerei des 15. Jahrhunderts", *Kunstwissenschaftliche Forschungen*, II, 1933, pp. 75-100, and Th. Rousseau, *op. cit.*

rigid warp of horizontals and verticals with interspersed diagonals is less exciting and the curves are incorporated with less spontaneity. The clashing movement of the two doors opened in opposite directions creates a discordant rhythm. The design as a whole is piecemeal and the shapes are grouped by an additive process without the volcanic force of the idea which inseparably welded them in A. The door in the background looks like an element deliberately composed within the V enclosure formed by the two donors. The small door and the standing man could hardly be visualized as having been there before the donor's wife was added, as was established by W. Suhr during restoration of the altarpiece, since they would have been jammed, unnecessarily close to the back of the donor. The silhouettes of the main figures here are sober and formal, whereas in A they show more imagination and poetic feeling. The hands play an important part in A, while here they are half-concealed by overlapping shapes.

A. Highly significant is the attitude toward the role of light as a stimulant of the mood. Light is unquestionably one of the decisive elements in the picture. It suffuses the sky as if emanating from the distance and enters the room from every direction. It is a cool, clean and precise light while the shadows cast tend to be warm and brownish in contrast.

The master was apparently fascinated by the shadows cast by various objects and represented them with intense interest. The phenomenon of the cast shadows expresses a mastering of reality or, more precisely, a resemblance to reality, since they represent an assembled notation of particular instances studied separately and are not seen as parts of an over-all light system. The master managed to use the independently observed shadows for the purpose of evoking an impression of daylight by placing them where they logically belonged. Some of the shadows are used for the solidification of the composition, while others add fancy as ornaments *per se*. These were undoubtedly already admired by the contemporaries of the artist, who manifestly took such a joy and pride in exhibiting some of the laws of projection, i.e. construction of shadow. He knew that the shadow is connected to its object at the point where the latter touches the projection plane and breaks each time a new plane is encountered.

The shadows fan out in triple and quadruple bunches and thus point to a multiple source of light. Such a scrutiny of the shadows shows us that it was the observation of artificial light that was the basis of his information. The edge of the vertical window frame on the right behind Joseph's bench casts a double shadow on the perpendicular wall, whereas in this arrangement the daylight alone would produce just a single shadow.

His observations of how the shadows cast by various objects behave when lighted by triple candlelight are brought together in the interior, which was constructed from separately perceived elements rather than as a real room objectively portrayed. This is confirmed by the fact that the shadows of persons are absent and the shadows of the architectural parts are very vague and incorrect whereas those of the objects are precise.

The exterior seen through the window of the shop is so thoroughly luminous that the shadows cast are practically eliminated as at high noon,[6] but the plasticity of the architecture is achieved by dark pockets of shadows underlining the projecting parts.

B.   There is no feeling of acute interest in the problem of atmospheric light. The daylight is soft, diffused and neutral to such a degree that it is not obvious from which direction it is coming. The light seems to be warmer than in the two other panels. The painter was oblivious of the existence of shadows, though the open gate offered him a wonderful opportunity for showing his mastery of shadows and brilliance of light. The few recorded shadows are anaemic and unconvincing. He was not aware of the fact that the objects and its shadow meet in the intersection of the two planes. The shadow cast by the door of the gate shows only an arbitrary shape which is not directly joined to the door.

The phenomenon of light and shadow does not create any conspicuous pattern in the composition and instead their importance is relinquished to the emphasis on light and dark surfaces considered more intellectually without much interplay, such as the Inghelbrechts couple against the background and the enclosure wall against the sky. The tiny houses in the street are modelled with the accent to a much lesser degree on dark shadows and they are consequently less plastic. The sides of the steps in the foreground are bluish instead of being distinctly shaded by a darker tone on one side as we would have expected by analogy with the architectural elements in the other two panels.

A.   The relief-like point of view has demanded an appropriate use of color. The colors are essentially treated as isolated phenomena and are applied to areas important from the standpoint of composition. These colored areas are not integrated by multiple links or color relation with their adjacent surfaces but are rather applied as a superstructure on a firmly elaborated ground form. These floating color shapes are anchored in a rather neutral surrounding which does not deviate much from a narrowly chromatic range. The right-hand wing especially may be viewed with some exaggeration as a painting "en camaïeu" on which bright and pure colors have been substituted in certain areas. Larger color surfaces, such as the red towel rack, the blue turban and Joseph's red sleeves, nevertheless, stand out without the least attempt at a chromatic optical blending.

There is also a discrepancy in the flesh parts, especially in the central panel.

6   The long shadows in the landscape in the Dijon Nativity are emphasized, as it happens, just before the sun, actually represented, goes down. This shows that the artist was interested in specific conditions of light.

The greyish tint of the hands would seem to belong to the restrained chromatic conception, whereas the faces are tinted with pink to raise them more to the expressive level of the colored surfaces of the robes. The hands suggest the painter's habit of using grisaille and show how much more at ease he was when he relegated the color to a mere surface coloring. Of course, the restraining of color is a necessary concession to the luminous conception prevailing here.

The view through the window is dominated by a more subtle and refined color instinct, and color here assumes the leading position held elsewhere by the chiselled sculptural form.

B. Here color is not viewed as an additive and independent factor.[7] It has been attenuated in order to permeate all forms, since powerful forms and powerful colors are antagonists. Color is directly involved in the very formation of the picture and is, in fact, a bearer of form and modelling, not simply serving as their striking embellishment. The interrelation and harmonization of color can be particularly well observed on the man standing by the gate.

The cool grey does not appear on the hands; on the contrary, the right-hand of the standing man is, in fact, painted a pronounced pink. The gamut of pinks on the masonry of the houses is quite different from that on the right-hand panel and has a tendency toward warm brownish pinks. The sky is less crystal-clear and does not turn blue toward the zenith.

The execution is consistently of a high quality throughout the triptych. The two methods of applying color cannot really be contrasted, for they are undoubtedly rooted in the same background and probably in the same workshop tradition.[8] However, some differences may be noted.

A. The infra-red light investigation discloses an amazingly accurate and purposeful preparatory drawing of every drapery fold of the angel's white robe consisting of fine hatching and cross-hatching. There are practically no deviations from the underdrawing in the final appearance of the drapery. The density of the paint of Mary's garment diminishes the visibility of the underdrawing, and yet that which is visible on the fabric spread on the floor shows the same meticulous virtuosity. It may also be observed on parts of Joseph's mantle. The appearance of the sharply drawn cross-hatching is that of an engraving. There is no underdrawing visible on the faces; only the right hand

---

7 Charles de Tolnay, "L'autel Mérode du Maître de Flémalle", *Gazette des Beaux-Arts,* Février 1959, p. 66 remarks: "Le fait que la composition et les couleurs des volets ne correspondent pas complètement entre elles paraît, à notre avis, avoir son origine dans un changement du projet pendant le travail". Yet I cannot agree with his proposition that the right-hand wing is the later of the two.

8 The tiny detail of red dots in the corner of the eyes may conceivably be taken as evidence of an indentical hand for A and B, but it may be, on the other hand, taken as a sophisticated, conscious desire for an identity of appearance.

of Mary is modelled by hatching. The underdrawing of the corbels supporting the beams of the ceiling is freer. Some pentimenti are even visible to the naked eye.[9] These minor corrections were made by the Master in a searching and uncompromising effort to attain perfection of form. His perfectionism went so far that he respaced the intervals of the holes in the fire-screen to achieve a more orderly and geometrical effect.

The X-ray photographs acquaint us intimately with the working procedure of the Master. Let us observe the technique used for the faces as the most revealing aspect of his approach. The construction of the paint layers appears to be a complex one and the volume is progressively built up by thin layers, starting with a stiff and "short" paint and establishing the main highlights in an economical manner. This first stage can be well observed in the face and hands of Joseph. The narrow strokes of paint containing lead white are distinctly visible, since the top layer contained very little white owing to the portrayal of a different, darker skin coloration from the light pinks of Mary's and the angel's faces.

On the other hand, the individual fine brushstrokes pre-establishing the basic highlights were concealed in the faces of Mary and the angel by a successive layer of light pink paint, rich in lead white and painting medium, forming an enamel-like, more homogenous "matière". The solid whites and deep hollows with practically no lead white on the X-ray produce dramatically lighted faces, yet they are, at the same time, soft and somewhat nebulous, because of the *sfumato* effect of their gradation.

If we compare the X-ray photograph with the painting, we are at once struck by a fundamental change in the countenance of the Virgin: her eyes were originally executed as not looking down but to the left.[10] The master originally portrayed the scene at the peak of dramatic action: the angel has just entered Mary's room and is at that very moment uttering the first word of his message

---

9   To the instances recorded by William Suhr, "The Restoration of the Merode Altarpiece", *The Metropolitan Museum of Art Bulletin,* 1957, p. 149, may be added: the beams of the left-hand portion of the ceiling, the curve of the display shelf in the right-hand wing, the receding line of the left-hand wall in the center panel and the prolongation of the front legs of the bench.

10   Originally, her head was slightly turned to the left. The original nostrils may be seen down and to the left of the present ones; the mouth was also placed to the left and slightly tilted; at the same time, the present left-hand outline of the face was slightly moved out of the original contour. The two chins recorded on the X-ray photograph give an impression of a cleft chin. The hair was first swept back on Mary's left temple, whereas the final version shows the hair hanging limply down. The drawing of her left eye, lower by a fraction than the other eye, as the head was slightly tilted in the mild torsion, seems to have been incised with a sharp instrument, as does also the hair in its upper right-hand portion.

(the gesture of his right hand shows that he has already started to speak). Mary upon hearing his voice has flashed her eyes in the direction of the coming voice, since at this moment of surprise, she has not had time to turn her head to spot the intruder. This is the highest moment of drama portrayed with a keen sense of psychological truth.

Why did Campin change this masterly acute interpretation of the spiritual encounter of these two beings who have suddenly met? We shall never know the true reason. I am taking the liberty of suggesting my interpretation, uncertain, though, as any attempt to disentangle a psychological problem is bound to be. The composition of his paintings shows Campin as a man with a powerful, dynamic and passionate mind, as can be seen from the Seilern triptych and the fragment of a large Deposition triptych in Frankfurt. His plastic language was loaded with great pathos and an expressive tension which, however, was not insensitive to poetic feeling. Yet the intellect of the painter deliberately imposed a controlling and moderating will on the spontaneous manifestation of this virile energy which, as a result, never permitted the dynamic tendency to get out of control. The master's solid and sculptural instinct, his disciplined desire for an absolute clarity and explicitness effectively counterbalances the innate exuberance. Consequently, we can only feel the tension and power of the form to expand in the dramatic and forceful configuration of the drapery, in the dynamic contours of the figures and the bold color. The motion of the design was deliberately immobilized by the introduction of static elements, and a monumental feeling was achieved.

By studying the dramatic effect of the original mood in the X-ray photographs I attempted to feel my way into the critical reactions of its author. I found it plausible that he may have felt that there was too much dramatic action and agitation in the picture, for he was striving for a pictorial statement of broader, slower rhythm and calmer mood. To extinguish one of the focusses of tension he perhaps decided to lower Mary's glance into her book in the more poised act of reading. The amended representation of the Virgin gained in tender and meditative qualities. However, the breaking of this oscillating spiritual contact brought a relaxation to the composition, at the expense of psychological veracity.

A slight reworking of Mary's features accompanied the alteration of her expression. The more angular jaw-line and more energetic chin composing her alert face was substituted by a quieter oval and doll-like face with a small feminine chin. Similar changes were introduced to the physiognomy of the angel. It was rounded out and made more ephebe-like; the front hairline was more elegantly arched to suit a contemporary ideal of the high forehead. His diadem was originally painted slightly higher and the back of his head was subsequently enlarged.

The X-ray examination furnishes us with a testimony of the artist's untiring search for a final statement of forms by improving upon the outlines.[11] The infatuation with precision can well be seen in the drawing of architectural elements, e.g. the white lines defining the complex profiles of the brackets of the ceiling look in the X-ray like an architect's blueprints. His obsession with the firmness of forms went so far that he traces the outlines of the double and triple cast shadows with a sharp white line. Their exactly determined shape is unlike the indistinctly and softly brushed-on shadows in the works of his followers and imitators. The view of the town houses becomes in the X-ray even more intense and hallucinatory and the plasticity of the draperies is striking.

Highly characteristic is the technique of scratching through the fresh paint layers as in *graffito* and working the paste with some pointed stick, used on the robe of Joseph, the wings of the angel and the half-timber of the houses on the market square. The disciplined impasto treatment of Joseph's hair which extends slightly under his headdress is likewise the manifestation of tactile values. Scratched into the half-dried paint are the bars and lead strips in the two round windows and the top of the workbench, boards and alignment of the nails on the floor in the right-hand wing.

B.   The infra-red radiation reveals none of the fine precision underdrawing of the folds that one would expect *per analogiam* at least in the white headdress enveloping the lady. Coarser and thicker cursorily drawn lines may, however, be perceived mainly in two areas, namely in the little house above the gate and the donor's head. The sketchy lines of the gatehouse are at variance with all its present proportions, as they had drawn a smaller structure.[12] The donor's face shows disconnected short, thick lines indicating features at variance with the visible ones. The ear was sketched slightly higher and closer to the cheek; a thick line on the upper lip, slantingly drawn, probably indicated the mouth; there are three curving lines across the present bridge of the nose which trace the original left eye and eyebrow; over the chin is a wide irregular stroke and another one draws the collar higher. The ensemble of these lines suggests that the face was originally somewhat smaller and more tilted up.

This manner of sketching shapes is diametrically opposed to that in the other two panels: in A the image of precision, in B unconcerned, approximate strokes, groping rather than knowing. There is a discrepancy between the careless tracing of lines which really are not intended to be followed and the precision of the finished image.

---

11   For example, the long hanging end of the angel's stole was made narrower, the edge of Mary's garment spread on the floor was more undulating and the house seen to the right of the workshop window had two of its windows concealed by the silhouette of the mullion, as it was made more robust.

12   The corbie-stepped gable, roof and window were placed lower, while the right corbel was drawn higher. Careless sketchy lines cross the house vertically on the right and continue down across the street.

The X-rays provide us with additional information on the lower layers of the donor's face. Separate strokes of a stiff paint which model the forehead and cheekbones in a circular movement are clearly visible. A smaller ear corresponding in position to the outline revealed by the infrared radiation is visible, and, in fact, it is clearer than the larger final form. There are two strong white patches on the ends of the C-shaped ear, but they seem rather to be parts of the final version. Any attempts here to reconstruct the original face must remain only tentative because of the incompleteness of the evidence.[13]

There is a much heavier layer of white on the lady's head, so that the brushwork of the features is but faintly visible. There are signs that both the head and the body were painted over the finished surface of the background and not on a reserved blank area (viz. the slight extension of the masonry underneath the veil).[14] It looks as if the area were covered with a layer of white paint to make the painting of the face easier by eliminating the disturbing effect of the painted background. The same thing also applies to a greater part of her body where the long sweeping brushstrokes disregard the conformation of the garment. In the area of the lady's mouth there is a disturbed scumble which belongs to a painting layer anterior to the painting of the face. The same seems to be true of a series of some eight, long, roughly parallel lines extending from the area of the ear to the right shoulder. A tiny figure was originally painted to the left of the horse and was subsequently overpainted.

A close examination of the X-ray photographs shows that the heads were not the only reworked areas. The shapes of both doors underwent slight changes as far as the height is concerned.[15] Portions of the flagstones forming the steps show an underpaint of dense white applied in long strokes, which is not functional from the standpoint of their lighting. Judging from the irregular application of the paint layers on the entire steps we may deduce that underneath them something else was concealed (which may have been, for example, the edge of a flowering lawn). A small curve in front of the bottom edge of the door and a long curve scratched upward across the bottom center reflect some scheme now unknown. The barely distinguishable shadows on the path seem to suggest that the edge of the man's garment was not exactly the same as we see it now.

---

13 The shadowy ridge cutting across the donor's forehead may perhaps be taken for the outline of the top of the previously painted head; its sketched features are visible with the infra-red rays. However, the earlier head seems not to have been pursued beyond the drawing stage with the exception of the ear.

14 The X-ray evidence corroborates the findings of Th. Rousseau and W. Suhr, *op. cit.*

15 The large door had a narrow slice added at the top while it was also elongated at the bottom—by some mm. It may, however, have been first sketched to reach considerably lower. The rows of nails have obviously been painted on only after the extension of the door.

The door in the gateway was also extended in its upper outline but was considerably shortened at the bottom, which reveals the experimentation and uncertainty of the painter in rendering perspective correctly. A few white tracing lines seem to indicate, though vaguely, that the right-hand house was first also intended to show its side-street façade. A shadowy jagged shape below it might have been a bush. It is not altogether certain whether the door in its present shape was a part of the original design and was perhaps meant to be wider. The curious lack of concern for luminosity in the area of the gate, which I have already pointed out, is revealed to be reversed in the X-ray picture. Some of the stones of the entrance wall were strongly lighted by a light coming from the right-hand background. The ashlar jambs of the gateway, now rather light, were on the contrary originally in shadow. The image of the little man at the door is unclear in the X-rays, which is surprising, since light surfaces, such as his stockings, would be expected to have a considerable white content to cover up the original painting of the masonry.

If we proceed with our minute examination to the left-hand top corner, we may perceive underneath the clouds architectural shapes recessing into space with an interesting outline of roofs, dormers and chimneys.[16] The light and shade on them was strongly indicated.

The amount of pentimenti in B is far greater than in A and reveals a fundamentally divergent idea of the conceiving and executing of a design. In A, the determined and purposeful creative mind never succumbs to wavering doubts about the basic correctness of the chosen design. He proceeds with an almost fanatical conviction, with only minor improvements, to materialize the statement of a pregnant idea. In B, a somewhat erratic tendency is revealed in a tentative formulation. The alteration of the donor's face (perhaps involving a change of identity), the addition of two figures and changes in the architecture are not mere improvements upon a lucidly premeditated design. There is little doubt that a second compositional scheme was superimposed. The door before its alteration, a single and possibly different donor, a large (?) open gateway, and tall houses on the left seem to belong to the first stage. I think that this scheme was never carried through to its full completion, as there are gaps in the application of the whites in the X-ray photographs. Some portions apparently were more advanced while others were perhaps left only in the drawing stage. This first composition may possibly be equated with the execution of the two other panels on the basis, firstly, of an affinity of precise brushwork, secondly, of an interest in luminosity exemplified in the painting of stones in the gateway and, finally, of the ghost architecture at the top. This architecture solidly braced the composition in a centripetal effect analogous to the compositions of A. The reworking of the donor, the added figures, the more

16   They may have looked somewhat like the roofs above the parapet at the top of an Annunciation in the Prado which belongs to the orbit of Campin's art. (See Appendix.)

fortuitous brushwork on the flagstones, the cruder handling of the highlights on the ironwork of the large door, the decoratively conceived plants and the monotonous masonry would be from a different hand.

It is even more in the domain of composition and surface patterns, in the attitude toward spatial depth, light, shade and color than in the actual execution that we observe differences of such a profound character that they can hardly be explained in terms of one artist's evolution.

However, if all the evidence submitted here is deemed by the critics inadequate evidence for recognizing in the triptych more than one artistic temperament, it would remain only to assume that the master abandoned his "reliefomania heresy", his enchantment with the magic of light and shade and the robustness of his conception of forms. The flame of his originality now extinct, he would have merged stylistically with his fellow artists of the younger generation. He would have grown tired of the acute observation of the structure and mechanics of things and would have retained only the superb rendering of the outer appearance of objects. He would have entered the evenly lit world where things were less exciting, where the drapery did not flow exuberantly and where people's movements had lost the spark of pathos. He would have assumed a less personal, more general attitude toward the composition and spatial construction, which, to be sure, shows some progress in the actual knowledge of receding space but, at the same time, is unable to control all the elements, thereby causing several lapses in the perspective. For the donors' wing has nothing of the exceptionality of A.

But even the slight falling-off in quality perceivable in B would be baffling, if nothing else, in the course of the artist's evolution. For instance, the lock, the doorknocker and, especially, the wall are rendered more superficially. The little houses and the actions of the tiny figures in the street are painted with less skill and imagination.[17] There is in A controlled vehemence and drama, whereas in B there is a cool, less decisive and less exciting performance which can be traced not only in the overall concept but also in the details. One has only to compare the difference in the renderings of the white linen protecting the Virgin's prayerbook and that enveloping the head of the lady donor. Or one may compare the sculptural bulkiness of the leaves of the lily and the thinness of the leaves of the rosebush. The weaknesses in composition of B have been mentioned above.

A certain thinness of the *état d'âme*, as it were, enters into the pictorial form of B, as can be observed in several details, and this is contrary to the virile and robust art of Campin. The silhouette of the donor's knees cuts abruptly into

17   They bring to mind, by comparison, the view into a town's street with shops and a similar horseman in the left-hand background of the panel representing St. Luke Painting the Virgin by Roger in the Museum of Fine Arts, Boston. Panofsky, *op. cit.*, Pl. 175, Fig. 313.

the path without that feeling for a spreading-out of the fabric on the ground in a supple play of folds which we see, for example, in the very same position on the Werl altarpiece wing in the Prado. This is only a symptom of his characteristic lack of drama.

The masonry in B is dull and the drawing of the pointing has something of a displeasing insistence about it. Its mechanical and repetitive character converts it from intense reality into an ornament *per se*. The architectural parts in A convey to us more of the excitement of their material existence. The herbs, though real species are represented, are combed into a pattern. The linear quality is heightened by the pattern of green grass shifting to the brown grass silhouetted against the steps.[18]

It would necessarily require a considerable lapse of time between A and B for the mental adjustment of the artist to the new conceptions to be possible, if one presumes that he painted both. It is illogical to assume that the donor's panel was the earliest and that the artist then shifted from the more advanced, painterly concept to the more archaic, yet stronger and more consistent conception which dominates the other two panels.

The differences can be explained better by assuming that two creative minds were involved, each with different outlooks and ideals but with the same artistic background. One was more powerful and original, the other more adaptable, more eclectic and smooth performer.

Campin's conception of space is fundamentally more archaic but is consistent in its outlook, so that it can be sensed almost as a true space. The other artist was more conscious of the new *vista* into the knowledge of space representation which was being opened at that time, but, although he was a perfectionist by nature, he was not yet able to master completely the new system. In any case, his knowledge of projection, i.e. his sense of perspective and the construction of cast-shadows, is inferior.

The motif of the donor witnessing the Annunciation through the opened door functions as an ingenious link between the two panels and bears a definite relationship to the same motif on the left-hand wing of the Werl altarpiece from 1438 in the Prado, attributed to the Master of Flémalle. In the latter, the design is more subtle, since the door opens in the other direction and there is not the startling foreshortening of the form reaching out of the picture plane. In the Merode altarpiece, the motif becomes a little too forced and too obvious in the effort to proclaim the unity of the two panels. In this instance, it seems as if the painter paraphrased this motif from the Werl altar-

18 This generalized decorative tendency becomes quite systematized in the gobelin-type grass in the Madonna of Humility in the Museum in Berlin-Dahlem. *Ibid.*, Fig. 198. A certain lifelessness contradicts its attribution to Campin. The motif of the grass silhouetted against the masonry occurs also in the Prado Betrothal and in Roger's early little Madonna in Lugano (Thyssen Coll.) and Daret's Presentation in Paris, Louvre.

piece. On the other hand, the latter work presents some problems as to its place among the other works of Campin, as will be shown later.

The whole spirit of the left-hand panel produces an impression of a painstaking desire to match the central panel. The painter tried hard to match the style but his own temperament and attitude toward the representation of space, light and color made it impossible for him to achieve a total stylistic identification. His art is less spontaneous, more careful and laborious in comparison with the more dramatic, straightforward and robust art of Campin. He did not share such conceptions as centrality and relief construction. An unfailing sense of design and visual rhythm suggested to the author of A an instinctive solution, whereas the author of B had to rely more on intellectual speculation. This resulted in some lapses, perhaps unavoidably so in view of the ambitious nature of the task. He showed a lack of capacity for devising some ingenious solution which would enable him to retain the deep and high field of vision without the necessity for disproportionately reducing some dimensions.

To bring the matter to a conclusion, we ask ourselves: why and under what circumstances? Here we are walking on the shifting sands of hypothesis, which may or may not supply a reasonable explanation of the discrepancies.

We can only attempt an explanation as to what the circumstances were which would account for the duality in conception. The ensemble indeed lacks symmetry in the Greek sense, i.e. any common module. My hypothesis is based on my impression from the X-rays that another face was originally sketched underneath; the changes occurred when the triptych changed hands or it was recommissioned before it had been completed. Then an associate of the master might have been commissioned to paint the new donor or rather owner and subsequently his wife. Unity in the appearance of the triptych was to be maintained. On this occasion, their coats-of-arms would have been painted on the upper tier of the window in the stained glass.[19]

The author of B probably belonged to a younger generation than the master of A and his panel in the finished state may be perhaps a decade or so later than the other two panels.[20]

19 It will, no doubt, never be known what was painted on the outer sides of the wings, for it seems highly improbable that such a precious ensemble would have been unadorned when the triptych was folded. Moreover, the original sizes of the three panels do not appear to have been fully preserved. It is interesting to note that not all the edges of the panels can be assumed for certain to be original; for instance, the right-hand edge of the left-hand wing appears to have been trimmed; the evidence on the right-hand wing is inconclusive. The lower and upper edges of all three panels are certainly original.

20 Dating based on costume is unreliable as the painter's or, possibly, sitter's conservatism may suggest too early a date. The hat in the donor's hands is not really the shaggy and semi-bulbous kind worn by G. Arnolfini and Baudouin de Lannoy in van Eyck's paintings but looks more like our nineteenth-century wide-brimmed hats. Similar forms seem to have been fashionable in the latter part of the reign of Philip the Good.

He possessed less individuality and his manner of thinking about the pictorial representation of space and the role of color and light was the same as that adopted officially, so to speak, by the Flemish post-Eyckian school.[21] For that matter, it tallies perfectly with our idea of the ideals embodied in the fifteenth-century Flemish painting.

21   The rendering of the little standing man appears to be Eyckian, owing to a softer quality of color application. The execution may also be compared with that of St. George on a small panel from the collection of Mrs. Impey in London, formerly in that of Lady Mason near Oxford. Emile Renders, *La solution du problème van der Weyden, Flémalle, Campin* (Bruges, 1932), vol. II, Pl. 6. In the Appendix, I shall dwell briefly on the question of the personalities of painters who participated on Campin's works and executed copies and replicas of the originals of his which are now lost.

CHAPTER II

The Entombment Triptych in London

Having ascertained that in the field of connoisseurship there still are some paths which have not been completely explored, I decided to study in detail the paintings attributed to Campin. I found myself fully in agreement with the findings of previous research that the earliest known of Campin's panel paintings is the Entombment triptych in the collection of Count Antoine Seilern in London. Elements of the composition, the types, their postures and dress, the color scheme, contain surprisingly eloquent hints of the future development of the master, although the whole is still archaic in comparison with any other of the works attributed to Campin. It is as if the triptych were announcing the whole range of his art but still in hesitant and undecided terms and not yet quite permeated with the later monumental breadth, greatness and beauty of form. When we compare the style with the contemporary Franco-Flemish panel production, alas, scantily preserved (such as the Martyrdom of St. Denis), it would seem possible to date the triptych as early as the first years of the second decade of the fifteenth century.

The triptych appears archaic in several technical aspects. First of all, there is the abstract gold background which tends to disappear in the Low Countries with the appearance of the new realistic school. It is adorned by a fine vine ornament individually shaped (not molded) in a low relief in the gesso to form a pattern which is slightly varied on each panel.[1] Secondly, the center panel is

1 The vine motif, favored in the plastic arts since late antiquity (Antioch chalice in the Cloisters) was revived in the Gothic period. This decor belonged to the repertory of

quite thick, unlike most fifteenth-century Flemish panels of comparable size. Thirdly, the panels composing the wings are carved from the same piece of wood as are the frames, with the exception of the top segments—a technical procedure which links these panels with the tradition of the preceding century.[2] Finally, the rounded arcade-like form of their tops may be a reminiscence of the sumptuous altar works embossed in gold.[3] The face of the angel hovering in the sky on the left belongs to the type before and around the turn of the century which were still unaffected by the new realism.

Color harmony in the three scenes is developed in a wide range of non-traditional combinations. A distinctive coloring enhances the various garments, some of which are made from the striped material for which the master had such a marked predilection.[4] Cool colors predominate and one can sense the painter's fondness for sandy colors which pervades not only the costumes (e.g. the kneeling Magdalen) but also the flesh parts. The sarcophagus is of an unusual light green color. Not only does the choice of color anticipate that found in Campin's subsequent paintings, but some of the physiognomies (the old man and Joseph) and postures (the woman seen from the back) are also prefigured here.[5] The paint is dense and massive and the highlighted folds on the kneeling woman's mantle, on the mantle of the right-hand angel and on

Mosan goldsmiths (a silver and copper gilt cross in the style of Hugo d'Oigny at Wildenstein and Co. in New York). It appeared only rarely in a raised pattern on Gothic panels such as on the Calvary of the Tanners in the St. Salvator's Museum in Bruges (Leo van Puyvelde, *La peinture flamande au siècle des van Eyck*, Brussels, 1953, p. 57 ff.) and on an Austrian Crucifixion in the J. Böhler Collection in Munich (Alfred Stange, *German Painting*, London, 1950, Pl. 43—ca. 1330).

2   Examples from the fifteenth century may be mentioned, e.g. a Pietà attributed to Jean Malouel in the Museum at Troyes (Grete Ring, *A Century of French Painting*, 1949, Fig. 28); Jan van Eyck's portrait of a Man in a Turban from 1433 in the National Gallery, London; Portrait of a Stout Man (R. de Masmines?) in the Thyssen Collection, in Lugano; and a portrait of a Man with Open Book by Roger van der Weyden in a London collection (F. Winkler, "Roger van der Weyden's Early Portraits", *The Art Quarterly*, 1950, p. 21 ff., Figs. 3 and 4).

3   Such as an ostensory with shutters in the Cologne Cathedral and a cross-triptych in the church of the Holy Cross in Liège from the twelfth century which is likewise adorned with a vine motif (*Trésors d'art de la vallée de la Meuse*, Exhibition in the Musée des Arts Décoratifs, Paris 1951, No. 84, Pl. 14). On the other hand, Kurt Bauch ("Ein Werk Robert Campins?", *Pantheon*, XVII, 1944, pp. 30-40) suggested as a possible source of the shape the Italian altarpieces such as those by Simone Martini and Taddeo di Bartolo. It is impossible to know whether the triptych when closed was also adorned with paintings on the outside.

4   Panofsky, *op. cit.*, p. 158.

5   Bauch, *op. cit.*, compared Veronica with the Suckling Madonna in Frankfort. The characteristic compositional device of upright aligned groups of forms, noted in the analysis of the Merode retable, already exists in the center panel; *vide* the vertical coupling of the kneeling Magdalen and the angel.

that of Christ are as if worked with a sharp stick. This manipulation of paint was observed in the Merode altarpiece.

The panels are a multiple testimony to the fact that Campin already had advanced on the route toward conquering realistic representation. The Magdalen's and John's hands and the bodies of the thieves foretell his later anatomical mastery, whereas other hands are still awkwardly drawn. The foreshortening of the face of the thief on the right can hardly be paralleled in any representation in Northern art at that time. The twists of the rope are studied with intense preoccupation and the multicolored flowers are individualized—yet not at the expense of the consistency of the meadow—as precursors of the glorious flora in the Frankfort panels. The Hebrew inscriptions adorning the garments are symptomatic of an attempt at historical accuracy.

On the other hand, some features are still rooted in the past. The terrain of the landscape in the left-hand wing is organized vertically rather than in depth. The road lined with wattle-fences and rows of trees does not recede into space as it does so wonderfully in the painting in Dijon. The rocks are still stiffly painted and still retain some of the prismatic facets, a time-honored practice.

A minute examination reveals that certain forms were treated in a somewhat different manner from the rest of the painting. They are characterized by a coarser handling, less sure brushwork, colors not so glowing, and less intensity of expression. This peculiar lack of intensity, so unlike the superb male figures on the center panel, is characteristic of the head of the donor and yet his hands are still consistent with Campin's manner. The head seems thus to be an alien intervention. The empty scroll painted over the trees, seems to be a further addition, the white paint of which is bubbly and coarser and does not have the usual enamel-like quality. The same less masterful hand may be recognized in two of the four angels holding the *arma Christi*, i.e. those on the left. The angel with a spear who is crowded and dwarfed into a narrow space appears probably to have been an afterthought. The concurrence of his left wing with the high headdress of Joseph of Arimathea is awkward compositionally. His face is merely grimacing when compared with the noble and silent grief of his counterpart on the right. His complexion is pale and bleak; the style is close to that of the Madonna of Humility in Berlin which I shall mention later. The angel in the sky on the left is definitely weaker than the one on the right. The difference in quality may be seen in the lack of plasticity of the face and the summary shape of the wings which are far below the studied anatomy of the bird-like wings of the other angel in the sky. It is probable that the master designed the drapery of the left-hand angel, so that the weaker hand may be seen only in the rendering. The face of Mary also seems to be inferior. It is coarser in execution and duller in coloring and, consequently, leads me to recognize there the hand of an assistant, although the type itself is very similar to the perfectly good face of Veronica. One more alien touch in the painting exists in the left hand of Christ which is too large and is malconnected to the wrist in addition to being too pink for the rest of the flesh. It produces an effect of an overpainting or a later completion by an unfinished hand.[6] I think that we have here a collaboration of two painters. It seems that the assistant was allowed to complete a few portions of the composition. He also painted the likeness of the donor. We may presume that occasionally some of the paintings would have been painted beforehand without a commission and offered to a prospective customer whose image was painted in when he purchased the picture.

6   It is possible that an examination by means of invisible radiation would elucidate the suspected relationship of the above-mentioned portions.

CHAPTER III

The Nativity in Dijon

It is the general opinion of art-historical research that the Betrothal of the Virgin in the Prado marks the following stage in Campin's evolution. I shall return later to a discussion of this panel, as it presents serious problems to my understanding of Campin's style.

It is in the Nativity in the museum in Dijon that a new vision, a new world comes into existence. The landscape is no longer a steep, up-turned and limited backdrop, but a vast expense has now opened up to the far horizon. We are led to believe through the suggestive effect of the authoritative spatial and color perspective that we could actually enter this space.[1] The little houses along the road are most convincingly realistic and bathed in the atmosphere of a particular time of a day in a manner so surprisingly modern that it is only paralleled in nineteenth century painting. The rendering of the landscape, especially its right-hand portion, attains the eminence of the "plein air" quality of the Milan-Turin Hours. It represents a radical break with the traditional vision and perception. We can today hardly imagine to what extent the first "peintres de la réalité" must have appeared supreme magicians to the admiring eyes of their contemporaries.

At the same time, the links with the past manner of Campin represented in

---

1   It is tempting to agree with the proposed identification of the distant town with the town of Huy on the river Meuse, but the water looks more like a lake than a river. Gaston Van Camp, "Le paysage de la Nativité du Maître de Flémalle à Dijon", *Revue belge d'archéologie et d'histoire de l'art*, XX, 1951, pp. 295-300.

his Entombment triptych are strong and unmistakable. The people, like actors, have stepped from a narrow and crowded stage on to the proscenium, and once they leave the distorting limelight they acquire a realer and more human appearance; yet they do not sever the ties which link them with their past roles. The very same types of people continue to haunt the painter's imagination; their features have the same kinds of configuration but are more refined. The very forms of their hands, eloquent and sensitive, grayish in color, betray their parentage. Campin's humanity is heavy, serious, robust, solemn, and never anecdotic or sweet. The figures seen from the back have not lost their previous stiffness entirely but their voluminous form is more complex and spatial. They still continue to fulfil their role of inviting the onlooker into the midst of the scene, but, at the same time, they assert the finiteness of the space represented in the forward direction from the projection plane. The X-ray photograph shows the same soft and gradual character in the building-up of the faces as was observed in the Merode triptych.[2]

The compositional pattern of clearly spelled-out forms, relief-like in character, well organized and avoiding any confusing overlapping, which we established as a salient feature of the center of the Merode and Seilern triptyches, may here again be recognized as a chief feature. The rhythm is curvilinear and energetic without becoming too exuberant or preciously elegant. The animated patterns of draperies and scrolls are counterbalanced by the placid landscape. The quiet mood of the distant landscape is, however, disrupted in the area of the rocky mountains at the top left. Their jerky and exaggerated rhythm stands apart from the overall, more poised rhythm. The main difference is that the jagged peaks are essentially unplastic, haphazard shapes lacking consummate formal sophistication, and their execution is less careful. In the same way, the pink manor house at the foot of the mountain has a more superficial form than the houses along the road on the right.

The X-ray photograph shows that the mountain peaks were originally less pointed and less crooked and that the modelling of the slopes was more realistic and logical. The steep slope to the right of the manor house now

---

2 Every color was carefully applied on a definite area without groping. As there is no dense white pigment in the minute gap between two colored planes, a dark thin line resembling a dark outline is recorded on the X-ray negative. It is significant that the underdrawing stage reveals the same purposeful brushstrokes in creating form, light and shade, as the final appearance was vividly present *a priori* in the artist's mind. The absence of the lead-white paint in the shadow cast by the little figures walking on the road shows that the shadow area was left uncovered by the brushstrokes painting the road; this indicates that the shadows were premeditated and not painted as an addition in the final stage. The dark tree-trunks were originally painted with a paint containing a considerable amount of white, more in fact than in the landscape around them, now light in tone. Here the white ground was used as a basic color reflected through thin layers of final color rendering.

seems to bulge because of its light surface and because the adjacent terrain forming a ridge right behind the manor is, against all expectation, dark. Originally, the transition between the large slope and the ridge was formed by a shaded gulf and the ridge was—much more logically—lighted. The peaks were originally highlighted to suggest their bulk.

The rate at which the objects in the landscape on the right diminish with their increasing distance is perhaps not absolutely correct but is always believable. This notion of a coherent system of spatial relationships is not fully realized in the left-hand background, as is demonstrated by the impossibly oversized tree painted in the middle of nowhere against the distant mountains which obviously belongs to a more recessed plane than the equally scaled trees in the center background.[3]

The colors in the upper left-hand corner of the landscape lack luminosity and are duller than elsewhere in the panel. A similar quality of dullness and routine unexciting treatment of paint may also be observed below on the adjacent thatched roof and this extends into the olive-brown area behind the group of shepherds. The muddy brown color lacks sparkle; it is smooth, dispassionate and slick. The brushstrokes reproduce the individual straws of the roof in a very general and superficial manner and the pattern of the tufts of thatching is monotonously repeated without variation or invention. The painter failed to reproduce their particular texture. This indifference, indicating a lack of interest in intense observation, was evident also in the donor's wing of the Merode triptych (e.g. the stone wall) and is to be contrasted with the marvelous representation of the dilapidated wall of the hut in the Nativity. Here Campin painted with delight the patches of mud and straw plastering on a grate of split reeds, which could not have been painted without actual study and observation. Truly, this is an infatuation with naturalistic detail of the same type as the rendering of the re-used wormy timber of the hut or of the carpenter's tools in Joseph's workshop in the Merode. Here then is manifest an apparent conviction about form, a tremendous perceptive power aiming at naturalistic individualization, an intense observation in the particular, which, however, owing to the genius of the master, does not disturb the essentially monumental character of his art.

On the other hand, there are a few parts such as the upper left corner, which show a tendency toward impersonal and abstract expression, elegant and smoothly painted but somewhat superficial. The choice of tonality is also different in both : Campin liked strong colors, juxtaposed and not integrated,

---

3 A similar lack of feeling for scale and its spatial implication may be seen in a similar example of an oversized tree perched on a mountain rock in the little painting with St. George from the collection of Mrs. Impey, London. (Emil Renders, *op. cit.*, vol. II, Pl. 8B) and also in the Nativity by Jacques Daret in the Thyssen Collection in Lugano-Castagnola.

almost dissonant in places, with cool tones predominating. The other painter (as I cannot possibly reconcile these basic differences with a single master) preferred less daring color matching, warmer harmony with a considerable amount of brown (cf. the color differences in the Merode retable).

The area of the roof is enlivened by a group of three angels on the left and a single angel hovering in front of the roof opening.[4] At a cursory glance they seem alike; for example the facial type of the angel at the extreme left appears to be identical with that of the single angel. Yet the execution of the former is less precise and less decisive, his flesh is more pinkish (cf. the weaker angel in the Seilern and the donors' hands in the Merode panels), and the paint is thinner; this is even more true of the other two in the group. These are the characteristics which we have observed in a few faces in the Seilern triptych. The wild, nonsensical conformation of the drapery approaches the spirit of the bizarre and jerky design of the mountains. On the other hand the lower end of the white drapery of the single angel has an expressive design tempered with a logical sense despite the fact that the tip end is restored. The drawing of the wings of the single angel shows a perfect understanding of their structure, which we may compare to the wings of the right angel in the sky of the Seilern Entombment. On the other hand the wing of the left angel is merely decorative; this time a parallel may be drawn with the angel holding the crown of thorns in the Seilern.[5] It is not surprising after appraising the differences in quality to find an incredibly awkward drawing of the hand of the left angel which is really nothing but a crippled tiny member, and is of course below the standards of Campin's imagination and craftmanship.

The distinct spirit of the three angels differing from the entire scene is particularly striking in the *coloris*. Three bright colors, red, blue and yellow of their robes are concentrated in a small area resulting in a vibrating effect but deflecting by their force the interest from the main scene. Particularly the yellow is out-of-tune with the general harmony and is not echoed in any other part. The painter evidently enjoyed the multiple play of colors. On the other hand the charecter of the colors in the main part of the picture is identical with that of *A* in our discussion of the Annunciation triptych. Each of the colors dominates a specific unit-form which is surrounded by areas of neutral colors which act as harmonizers and prevent dissonances. This cool harmony of the master is opposed to the warmer harmony of the other painter.

4   A triad of angels also exists in Daret's Nativity and Roger van der Weyden's Bladelin altarpiece.

5   We may also distinguish, if we make a close scrutiny of the X-ray photograph, two sets of distinct brushwork in the two scrolls held by the angels, one drier, the other more softly sensuous. The left-hand scroll is more yellow under ordinary light and the letters of the inscription are more ordinary and impersonal than the truly calligraphic letters on the other three scrolls.

Morphological analysis shows that an all-embracing identical treatment was not accorded to all details with the same intensity, and differences may be observed also in the drawing. Let us be more specific. The hands are important in the pattern of the painting, their sensitively drawn shape with articulated joints is expressive and the nervous vibrating fingers evoke elegance in the feminine hands—the very type we have seen in the Merode retable. Not all the hands are conceived in this way: the hand of the left-hand shepherd is inferior in its claw-like form, the uninteresting tapering sticklike fingers lack impasto wrinkels on the knuckles. It is rather pink with dull brownish shading, whereas the other representations (except the angels on the left, of course) are grayish or pale with typically cool shadows.

The intervention of the unknown helper does not seem to be restricted to compact areas which conceivably might have been left unfinished or only sketched out. It also appears sporadically in places which had, as a whole, been brought to a state of perfection by the Master himself.[6] The strong design of the lower right-hand corner is marred by a change made in the posture of the half-kneeling woman. Her feet are concealed by a precious heavy fabric decorated with ornamental bands alternating with Hebrew inscriptions which is wrapped inside-out around the lower part of her body. We can only guess their exact position, and yet their invisibility is not disturbing and is, moreover, justified for compositional and rhythmical reasons. Apparently, this somewhat indistinct conformation was found unsatisfactory by the continuator and he appended the right leg to the skirt. This "correction" proved to be a failure both esthetically and anatomically.

The observation about an alien intervention is confirmed by examination with infra-red rays. Under this illumination certain areas are shown unjustifiably darker. Their indistinct outlines suggest that a flat dark underpainting may have been applied here which had no relation to the actual forms represented. This would be a peculiar deviation from the rest of the painting.[7] It occurs in the upper left-hand area of the mountains, including the manor and the road-side inn (?), in the leg appended to the kneeling woman just

6 I am inclined to think that there was hardly such a tight cluster of shepherds in the original design and that the middle figure was added by the assistant along with the two hands resting on the shoulders, while the hand clutching the spear might have originally belonged to the left-hand shepherd. It also must be noted that the face with teeth showing in the mouth has analogies in the Madrid Betrothal and in a saint's fragment in the Gulbenkian Collection in Lisbon which belongs to the reading Magdalen in London (see further). With regard to the un-Campinesque types of the two shepherds K. Bauch writes (op. cit., p. 40): "... Züge und Partien die unmittelbar nach Roger aussehen. Schon in Dijon gibt es unter den Hirten ..."

7 The darker, scumbled-on lower layer, though highly untypical, would not in itself be a proof of a different hand, but, as cumulative supporting evidence, it corroborates other observations made by the naked eye and under raking light.

mentioned and in a patch underlying the church. In fact, this building is drawn in a much steeper perspective than the rest of the town and traced more harshly, without regard for an atmospheric mellowing of the sharp lines.

If we attempt to evaluate the role and meaning of the portions which we have found to be additions or changes in terms of the entire composition, we may characterize these changes as confusing the clarity of the scene, crowding some areas and bringing about a pedantic balance of certain elements, the result being a loss of pictorial expressiveness.[8] We may gain the impression that the second hand was a continuator and collaborator rather than strictly a subordinate helper. For his additions reveal the self-assurance and conviction that he could improve upon the other artist's composition in general and amend details which he judged to be insufficient or lacking (viz. the right foot of the kneeling woman). I think that an analogous relationship existed in the Seilern triptych (viz. the left-hand angel). The question as to the reason for the collaboration must remain unanswered—was the master prevented by a *force majeure* from finishing the panel, did he decide not to finish it or did he delegate its completion to his close associate.

8   The cumulative tendency may be demonstrated in the case of the three shepherds where two would have sufficed to animate the center of the scene. The added group of angels on the left weakens the concentration and emphasis on the main figures and brings the restless and turbulent shapes into an area which was probably intended to make its impact solely by means of the broad architectural forms of the roof. It is possible that there was in the original design a traditional dormer-window in *lieu* of the hovering triad of angels, which, however, could hardly be brought beyond the stage of a mere underdrawing, since there is no indication on the X-ray of any *pentimenti*.

CHAPTER IV

The Virgin and Child in London

The Suckling Madonna in the National Gallery in London, known as the Virgin and Child before a Fire-screen or the Salting Madonna, belongs to the same period as the Nativity and the Merode triptych. I shall attempt by means of an analysis and interpretation of the pictorial phenomena to clarify the relative position of the panel within the chronology of the triad.[1]

On the basis of the chromatic values we can see more similarity between the Merode and Dijon paintings, the London panel being different from both. In the first two, the painter's fascination for strong and pure local colors may be felt, as we have suggested in the analysis of the Merode retable, while color harmonies less daring and of a narrower range are used in the London panel. Here the coloring of the figures and the interior does not produce any strong color emotion; the painter seems to have been more preoccupied with expressing the light values than with shapes as bearers of individual and pronounced color qualities. The radiant colors of the Merode Annunciation are absent (with the exception of the ultramarine sleeves to be discussed later). The artist tuned his color harmony to a balanced accord of red madder and green (the cushion and the hanging cloth) with supporting neutral colors.[2] The red-blue

1 There is an indication, however, that examination from various aspects, such as the composition, drawing, representation of space, realism, color and brushwork, does not produce the same conclusions and thus varies the tentative sequence of these three panels.

2 The X-ray shows a tongue of flame appearing just off the lower left-hand edge of the fire-screen which is not apparent on the surface. Likewise, a forged finial iron of

scheme of the Merode Annunciation is more emphatic and the variety of strong, pronounced colors is richer. There are, however, many concurrences in the Merode and London panels; for example, the green on the bookpouch in the Annunciation is identical to that used on the pillow in the London painting and the sandy hue of the three-legged stool resembles the color of the furniture in the Merode triptych. Hair in both works is rendered in a cool harmony of raw umber and light yellow lustre; flesh parts also tend to have cool tints. This testifies to the persistence of the color vision of the master. However, the dull subdued red of the lips on the London figures has less vitality than the fresh sanguine lips of the Annunciation.

Both the robe and mantle of the Salting Madonna are apparently of the same woolly white material and are shaded with a violetish ultramarine, whereas the angel's garment in the Annunciation is shaded with a cooler ultramarine blue. In contrast, the white linen under the child and under the book in the London painting as well as that protecting the book in the Annunciation are shaded in gray and this diverse degradation of whites adds a refined quality to the whole harmony. The gray with a slight greenish cast of the furred lining of the cloak of the London Madonna is perhaps a little too subtle and subdued a color harmony with the white of the cloak. It shows how far the painter was already removed from the vivid coloristic taste prevailing in the works of the International Style flourishing in the early fifteenth century. His delight in the tactile impasto treatment of some details led him to apply small lumps of white paint on the tiles and on the highlights of the cloak.[3]

The most refined color sense, however, was reserved for a comparatively small area of the luminous vista through the window. The gate is a warm brownish pink; the colors of the houses are variegated with ingeniously organized pinks, whites and bluish grays; the tiny church is *ajouré* with a white filigree impasto. The landscape behind the town is painted in sienna, a favorite color with the master, as we have seen in the landscape in the Dijon Nativity. The hills rising in the background are bluish and the ensemble achieves a rare spatial and color perspective.

If we wished to hypothesize that Campin's color perception evolved toward increasingly pure and distinct colors applied in larger and larger areas, we would be led to conclude that the London panel is an earlier work than either the Merode or the Dijon paintings. On the other hand, there is the possibility that Campin's later work was in a more restrained range of colors. Fortunately, criteria other than color enter here and help us determine the chronology.

---

a pole in the axis of the screen is not visible. This suggests that the background wall was repainted in a dark, almost black color, which obviously has a muffling effect on the whole color harmony.

3   Martin Davies, *Les primitifs flamands; 3. The National Gallery London* (Antwerp, 1953), Pl. CXIV.

Furthermore, certain areas were altered, thus possibly changing considerably an earlier scheme to a different color mood (the almost black repaint of the wall and other portions to be discussed later).

There is an archaic quality in the London panel produced by the awkward perspective and the strangely proportioned figure of Mary. She is short and stocky and her large head on a powerful neck produces an almost monstrous effect. The awkward left arm, as wrongly reconstructed on the strip of wood added to the panel, even accentuates the width of the massive body. The excessive prolongation of the nose, which together with the large eye-lids dwarfs the rest of the face, seems to indicate at the first glance an early period when Campin still had not mastered a realistic harmony of facial proportions.

The study of X-ray photographs proves very helpful in trying to discover the original concept of Campin. We thus learn that the mask-like effect of the face only is really a product of the final layer of painting. The underpainting reveals a somewhat more satisfactorily proportioned face, i.e. the temples were originally higher, being later reduced by bringing the hairline closer to the eyes. The original features resembled even more closely those of the Virgin in the Merode Annunciation and—as we shall see later—also those of the fainting Mary in the Deposition from the Escorial.

The X-ray furthermore shows that Campin originally envisaged less opulent hair, for the wicker pattern of the fire-screen was painted closer to Mary's head. The modelling of the face is less "empâté" with white than in the Merode triptych. There is an unblurred precision in the drawing of the mouth, nose and eyes. The lighted areas of the volumes were built up consistently without hesitation. The hands too are accurately modelled and the precise shape of the nails was already determined, as were many other details, in the first stage of painting. Likewise, the lock crowning the forehead of the Child was already envisaged in the beginning of the execution, as the absence of the white layer at that spot demonstrates. Shading, modelling and placing of details were inseparable and not consecutive phases in the painting process of Campin. The fine "lines" which appear to outline many forms are, in fact, spaces left between two areas of paint, so precise was the application of the paint in two neighboring areas. All these qualities are characteristic of the clear-minded, determined working method of the painter.[4]

4   The boldness in the execution does not exclude a striving for the perfection of shapes, as is shown by a few alterations such as the shifting of the Child's left nipple sidewise, the lowering of the outline of his right thigh, and the widening of the Virgin's right thumb and of the back rest of the bench. It must be conceded that Roger's painting procedure is similar in some of his works, as these dark "precision lines" appear on the X-ray photographs of his Christ Appearing to the Virgin in the Metropolitan Museum of Art (A. Burroughs, "Campin and van der Weyden Again", *Metropolitan Museum Studies*, 1933, pp. 131-150, Fig. 5) and in the Lamentation in the National Gallery in London (ex-coll. Earl of Powis).

In contrast with the archaic quality of the facial features and the sculptural relief-like deploying of the cloak on the ground is the suggestion of space extending from the bench through the window into the distant view of the landscape. It is achieved by a clear articulation of parallelly set planes and a vivid and true effect of atmosphere, despite the contracted steep perspective. Light glides quite realistically over the back of the bench, the armrest with the carved lions and the cushion and creates a complex pattern of light and dark zones. This recreation of space, notwithstanding the remnants of conventional spatial organization, represents a remarkable and advanced achievement—the work of a genius.

With the help of X-rays we may gain some insight into the creative processes. Clearly visible is the alteration of both sleeves of Mary's mantle. The right sleeve did not originally have the deep transverse folds and its silhouette was simpler and more slender. The length of the sleeve was not altered but originally lacked the fur cuff. Now, we have explained why the furry lining on the sleeve and on the cloak further down are not of an identical hue. The left sleeve was wider and more diagonally placed, bringing Mary's elbow much nearer to her body.

More significant and psychologically interesting are other changes in the same area. First of all, we may perceive that originally Mary's white shirt reappeared from under the sleeve of her robe, which was quite wide, recalling the sleeves of Mary in the Annunciation. The shirt sleeve was long and tight and its funnel-like ending covered one-third of her right hand. It is thus established that the ultramarine of the robe sleeves belongs only to the changed scheme. Why were these changes made? Now, the narrow and tight sleeve concealing part of the hand was a conservative feature in fifteenth-century dress. This fashion was current throughout the second half of the fourteenth century, as many illuminations show us, and was rarely depicted after the first quarter of the fifteenth century.[5] On the other hand, typical of the fifteenth century is the fashion of a separate sleeve, often made of a brocaded material differing from the rest of the robe and fastened at the shoulder with a pin.[6] It would seem that the reason for the alteration was to bring the old-fashioned sleeves up-to-date rather than to improve the design for artistic reasons.

The latter consideration probably was responsible for the radical redesigning of the feet of the Christ child and the linen under his body. The right foot was placed lower and made larger, while the thigh line and knee were lowered.

5   See, for instance, MS XVII A 6 in the University Library in Prague from 1376. Dating on the basis of costume is, however, a tricky business, as this sleeve appears as late as 1479 in Memling's painting, Mystical Marriage of St. Catherine, in Bruges, Hôpital Saint-Jean.

6   Cf. the sleeve fastened with a pin on the shoulder of the Magdalen in the Bracque triptych in the Louvre and on the extreme right of the Escorial Descent.

The *pentimento* in the left foot looks as if it were also smaller. The linen was originally more ample and laid in a different way.[7]

A very important change is the shifting in the direction of the Child's look. The X-ray photograph clearly shows that the Child was looking to the left, whereas the final rendering shows him looking straight out of the picture toward the spectator.[8] The original intense look seems to indicate that the Child was looking at someone present in the room to the left of the Virgin. The direction of the look would indicate that it was a kneeling figure rather than a standing one. Was it a donor adoring the Child, or a saint?[9] The per-

7   It was spread over Mary's left knee, while the Child's left heel pressed into it a series of converging folds. The edge of the loose overhanging portion continued upward diagonally, passing Mary's wrist, and concealed a little more of his left hip. Then the rest of the fabric fell over her forearm in vertical folds, the form of which was partly retained in the revised final version. It also partly concealed his right knee. It seems to me that the small crumpled folds producing a jerky movement along the Child's side were not a part of the original design. The X-ray photograph, unfortunately, stops at the right-hand edge of the white covering of the book, the draping of which also underwent a change. Its edge once fell over the Virgin's sleeve and it may be that the whole sheet was substantially changed.

8   We must remember at this point the changes in the look of Mary in the Merode Annunciation.

9   It seems to me that I can faintly perceive an uncertain object (flower?) held upright in the left hand of the Child. If this is so, this would make sense of a now meaningless gesture. I would like to offer a few hypothetical explanations concerning the change in the iconography. It may be that the commissioner who desired to be portrayed in the painting died before Campin completed it or that the contract was cancelled for some reason. Campin, consequently, would have made the right half of the diptych a selfcontained scene by changing the direction of the Child's gaze to make the composition psychologically complete and capable of existence as a single panel. It may be also that he never got around to the task of painting the figure which aroused the interest of the Child in the original scene. Finally, it may be that the alteration was made by an associate of Campin.

The assumption of a more complex composition is based also on the existence of a Campinesque composition which is known only from a late XV century copy preserved in the convent of the Poor Clares at Puy de Dome. (Vitale Bloch, "An Unknown Composition by the Master of Flémalle", *The Burlington Magazine,* vol. CV; Febr. 1963, p. 72 f.). The large canvas (207 x 181) represents the Holy Family. Joseph at the left is peeling an apple for which the Christchild is reaching with His hand. Many details of the setting, garments, and gestures can be paralleled in the Salting Madonna in London; those of the gestures and garments in the Frankfort Madonna and in the Madonna with Saints in Washington; the type of the angel can be compared to that in the Louvain Trinity.

Considerable portions of the painting were cut at the right side and the top. The size of the lost parts is difficult to estimate. It is conceivable that the window was originally represented somewhat taller. A large section at the right was reconstructed in the XIX century. However, the reconstruction contains some elements of fancy. The narrow customary rim of bare wood at the bottom is missing but the pattern of large tiles alter-

spective of the floor with its vanishing point wavering in the area below the window-sill would acquire more meaning if another substantial part of the floor with tiles sharply converging to the right could be assumed. Could the painting of the nursing Madonna have been the right-hand half of a diptych with the kneeling donor on its left-hand half?

The brushwork in the areas which were singled out here as showing *pentimenti* or changes in scheme is similar, in general, to that in the rest of the painting. All indications seem to suggest that all the alterations were made by Campin himself. However, I should like to dwell on the whole complex from a different angle, the artistic one. We must admit that the area around the Child's feet and his side has been changed for the worse, at least from the standpoint of naturalism. A stiffly traced, slightly inclined line of the knee was substituted for a more organic and naturalistic design in which the drapery gave way to the pressure of the Child's heel. Further to the right, the linen conformation, stiffened and crumpled as if starched, originally fell again in a big sweep, as on the other side, over the Virgin's forearm. My interpretation of the X-rayed brushstrokes in the area of her left hand, which is, one must admit, particularly difficult to prove, may be yet another instance of the rejection of a more realistic solution. A smaller hand which would have been better proportioned in relation to the right hand seems to have been first painted in a functional gesture of actually supporting the Child. The present hand is laid flat palm-up beside the Child's thigh instead of supporting it, whereas in the original position the hand appears to have adhered to his thigh in the holding pose. It is difficult to conceive that a painter who testified throughout his work to an intense interest in realism would eliminate an excellently observed notation of the real in favor of an arbitrary and lifeless form. A possible explanation that he was perhaps concerned with the simplification of the forms does not ring true when we see that he proceeded at the same time to multiply the drapery scheme of the sleeve and the little folds of the white linen.[10]

It is difficult to decide whether the changes were made during the execution of the painting itself or resulted from some subsequent intervention. Evidence

---

nating with four small ones, analogous to the floor in the Merode Annunciation, indicates that the lower edge could have been trimmed only very slightly. The photograph in M. Davies, *op. cit.,* pl. CXLIV, shows the unpainted left rim and on p. 66 it is stated that the edge is the original one.

10   The irregular and more superficial execution of the floor tiles on the left below the stool is also puzzling. A couple of tiles stand out of the ensemble, and the pattern of alternating large octogonal tiles with a sequence of small rectangular ones, as it exists in the front row, is as if forgotten in this area. It seems strange that the painter should forget the exact appearance of shapes and pattern he himself had devised—especially a man who was concerned so much with the inner structure, mechanism and logic of the appearance of things. Is it not rather an area of an old repaint by some other hand?

pointing to the latter seems to lie in the changed shapes of the sleeves. Whoever made the change seems to have been conscious of the current taste. It is highly interesting that an alteration may also be detected on the sleeves of Veronica in Frankfort, where a brocade pattern was repainted plain blue, as I shall show later in my discussion.

In conclusion, we may observe that a certain frontality of planes and archaic facial features would put the painting prior to the Merode Annunciation. However, it may be that the London painting was created over a period of years and that certain more advanced and refined features such as the atmospheric perspective were executed in the years following the completion of the Merode triptych.[11] In any case, it seems to me that the *finished* work would postdate the Merode painting.

11   Jules Destrée published in the *Connoisseur*, 1926, p. 209 f., a mediocre copy in the collection of Madame Reboux in Roubaix. Though faithful in general, it differs in some points. The late fifteenth-century copyist shifted Mary's head from the strictly frontal view to a position somewhat to the left. It is interesting to note that an identical change was made to Mary's head in the replica of the Merode Annunciation in Brussels. Was it an expressed disapproval of the frontally staring and archaic mien of the figure? A cupboard on the right, though much simpler, shows that the restorer of the Salting Madonna must have had some notion of the existence of this portion which perhaps was sawn off because of its decayed support and replaced by a new piece. The sheet under the Child is more richly draped and conceals his feet. The kerchief around the neck of the Virgin is a rather insignificant addition. More important is the omission of the view of the town, which was substituted by heraldic emblems in the stained glass. Finally, the perspective of the arm-rest is such that its rear end comes just under the left corner of the window. This two-dimensional and more geometrically conceived design is more in keeping with the archaic drawing of the Virgin's pose itself and with the whole composition, for it avoids any excessive spatial implication, which is so startlingly advanced in the London original in precisely this area. If *pentimento* could be detected there, it would show that a copy was perhaps made in the early stage of the painting, subsequently recopied in the Roubaix picture, which recorded the situation before its improvement by a more naturalistic and atmospheric rendering of the bench and the window.

CHAPTER V

The Four Panels in Frankfort

(Madonna, Veronica, Trinity, Thief on the Cross)

The mature style of Robert Campin is epitomized in the four panels in the Städelsches Kunstinstitut in Frankfort. Two panels with the standing Madonna and Veronica seem to belong together as wings of a large altarpiece. The third panel with the Trinity in *grisaille* was probably once the reverse of the Veronica panel. The fourth large panel is a fragment of a still larger altarpiece. This upper portion of the right-hand wing represents the bad (?) thief on the cross and two soldiers apparently gazing on the Crucified Christ on the lost centerpiece.[1]

Mary and Veronica stand against the backdrop of two different, luxuriously colorful heavy fabrics and their feet are planted in a dense growth of naturalistically portrayed flora. The multicolored Lucchese brocades seem to hang on the wall, as part of it may be seen in the gap between tapestry hem and the lawn. Thus the space is deliberately curtailed to a shallow proscenium. The splendid decorative effect of the panels is heightened by a *fortissimo* coloring in which the contrasting colors do not rival each other, being rather ingeniously arranged and proportioned, each retaining its brilliant appeal. Veronica's body silhouettes as a dark crimson red mass against the pale grayish sky blue of the backdrop fabric which is enlivened with small accents of bright colors. Conversely, the light figure of Mary is contrasted against the darker intense colors

1 A mediocre copy of the whole altarpiece is in the Walker Art Gallery in Liverpool. Panofsky, *op. cit.,* Fig. 230. The composition of the Deposition was repeated in a sixteenth-century triptych in the cathedral of Segovia.

of the fabric hanging behind her. One of the glories of the paintings is the superb rendering of the lush vegetation. The decorative quality of this floral carpet is not achieved by schematization and stylization: on the contrary, the various plants are painted most realistically in their material and tangible substance and can be easily identified.[2] The refined differentiation is achieved even in the *coloris*, as some plants are more indigo blue in their green and others more warm green.

The paint is applied throughout in massive and solid layers. The paint on the end of the Madonna's cloak spread on the grass even assumes a relief quality. The white was applied by stippling in little impasto dabs, and the texture of the paint in the shadows almost suggests the brushstrokes of the impressionists. The thick application of the paint has been noted already in the above analysis of the Merode triptych as a hallmark of Campin's technique. The subtle *coloris* of the Mary's clothes recalls the seated Mary in London. A thin red belt cuts through the ultramarine blue of the Child's garment and thus brings a tension and excitement to the area. The fur on his collar and cuffs is in a cool gray with a greenish tinge, analogous to the lining of the Mary's mantle in London. This silvery tone is one of the subtle variations on the theme of cool tones dear to Campin.

The left hand of Mary in Frankfort and the right hand in London are very similar, as are also the neck openings of the two dresses. The volume of her breast was expressed in the same manner in both instances. A kinship exists between the two faces, but in Frankfort it is better proportioned and gives the impression of being a more advanced work. The stylistic similarity between the London and Frankfort representations of the Virgin may be further substantiated by a striking similarity in the features of the two representations of the Child. The particular shape of the slightly upturned nose and the shape of the ear are the same in both. The likeness of the two heads is still greater, if we compare the underlying forms of the Child's head in London as revealed by the X-rays. There his countenance assumes a more mature and serious look —like the Frankfort Child—according to the traditional representation of the Child as a little grown-up. A slight reworking of the London head changed his expression to a more child-like one. If we assume that Campin himself made the change, then we must conclude that this alteration, and that of the Virgin's sleeves for that matter, date from after the execution of the Frankfort panel. The X-rays show also that his head was originally more elongated, which would have made him resemble even more the Child in Frankfort. Its back bulged as far as to his ring-finger.

The X-ray photograph of the upper part of the Madonna shows an uplifted face in the area of her neck. It is the face of a Mater Dolorosa painted on the

2   Some sixteen plants are identified in Lottlisa Behling's *Die Pflanze in der mittelalterlichen Tafelmalerei* (Weimar, 1957), Pls. XLII-XLV.

reverse of the panel which is in a poor condition of preservation. However, a close scrutiny of the X-rayed features discloses that the original face was concealed by a crude repainting which generally followed the original disposition of the face but not that of the veil. The modelling of the nose and the brushwork of the eye on the left (the other eye is indistinct beneath the thick layer of white used for shaping the Madonna's breasts) accords with Campin's technique, and is far superior to that in the repainted stage, which is highly insensitive in form. There is even a highlight on the eye, which shows that the face was completely finished. The brushstroke curving down across the tip of the Madonna's chin and continuing across the lower portion of the Child's face on the shadowgraph is in fact the edge of the original veil of the Mater Dolorosa. The line of the cloak-hood repainted in a Baroque fashion may be perceived cutting across the Madonna's neck and her veil. It seems from the *pentimenti* on the Madonna's left cheek that the original veil was provided with ruffled edges. The evidence of the master's idioms substantiates the feeling that a damaged painting of a Mater Dolorosa by Campin on the reverse of the panel was at a considerably later period repainted and partly changed. The form of the socle also seems to lead to this conclusion.

It is difficult to decipher the *pentimenti* on the lower portion of the Madonna's breast: a circular form which recalls the nipple seems to suggest that the breast was originally drawn in a frontal position resembling that in London. It appears also that the edge of her collar was first drawn differently. *Pentimento* in the area of the Child's right hand suggest that the hand was perhaps only an after-thought. Furthermore, it is possible to interpret the brushwork in the area of the Madonna's eyes (especially the right one) as representing the eyes originally looking straight out of the picture. This change from a straight to a down-cast gaze would then coincide with the change in Mary's countenance in the Merode Annunciation and be related in nature to the changes in the Child's eyes in the London panel.[3]

The style, technique and mood are constant throughout the painting and indicate that the painting remains unaltered by any alien intervention.

This is not the case in the companion panel representing Veronica. Her body, fabric backdrop and the beautifully painted grass are one homogeneous whole unmistakenly by Campin's hand. His bold brushwork can clearly be discerned and the red of the garment and the deeper madder red shadow areas have a deep, glowing and rich quality. The rendering of the borders studded with

---

3 These changes are symptoms of a truly creative approach and contradict the concept of Campin's artistic personality as hesitant and uncertain, as put forward by Burroughs (*op. cit.*). Compare a working procedure of the highest intellectual order as seen in the work of Jan van Eyck, such as in his Arnolfini Marriage and the Madonna of Canon Van der Paele (Jules Desneux, "Underdrawings and Pentimenti in the Pictures of Jan van Eyck", *The Art Bulletin*, March 1958, pp. 13-21).

precious stones is like that of Salome in the Dijon Nativity and the studded haloes on the standing Madonna panel. We may notice the stylistic and technical discord when we look at the focal point, i.e. the head. The worried face of an older woman is utterly incongruous with the youthful pose of her body. It is not simply that it is too large, because we have already noticed such a discrepancy in the London panel (and we must not forget that this is only the beginning of experimentation in naturalism in the new era of painting); it is, more than anything else, the formal and psychological incompatibility. It is as if this gracious woman, thus identified by her elegant stance, has disguised herself with a large face-mask.[4] The sinuous S-curve movement is deadened by painstakingly descriptive and sentimental notation of an older matron's face. We would expect as a culmination of this elegant body movement a different, younger face which would harmonize with the posture and gesture of the figure.

The chromatic effect of the head differs from other works of Campin. The bold appeal of strong, juxtaposed colors, each calculated not to interfere with the effectiveness of the other, is not found here. Instead, an ineffectively narrow blue of a ribbon near the collar and another insignificant color accent in the orientalizing hair covering, made much too complex by a superfluous transparent veil, are too weak and become submerged optically in the larger areas. These "accents" appear as cautious afterthoughts. The eyes are of a rather untypical warm hazy brown-green hue and lack an intensity of expression, which reminds one of the eyes of the Child in the London panel. The color of the complexion is unlike all flesh tones in other Campin paintings. The pink has a violetish and impure quality which suggests a different combination of the pigments; perhaps a different and coarser red pigment was mixed with the black and white as a basic combination. The shadows are warm. The X-rays reveal that the white was admixed only in small proportions into the top flesh layer, as can be inferred from the more simple stratification. The clearly delineated highlights were applied in the lower layer.

The hands of Veronica are quite different from the hands of the Virgin on the companion panel. The skin envelops the flesh tightly without wrinkling, which makes the hands slightly swollen. Their generalized and idealized shape contrasts with the intensely naturalistic and individualized hands of typical Campin figures, whose highly articulated, knuckly fingers are sensitively

4   The painstaking realization of the shapes and minute planes suggests that the face was closely copied from a preparatory scale-drawing or cartoon, whereas genuine Campinesque faces are much more painterly and less linear. They were deeply imprinted in the master's mind and therefore did not have to be slavishly dependent on a preliminary highly studied drawing. There are losses in the paint along the crack running through the face, e.g. one half of the lips is new. Other losses are in the kerchief and in the background.

drawn. Veronica's nails conform in their shape to that of the finger tips, while those of Campin are more convex, so that they sink on either side into the flesh which bulges around them. (Let us bear in mind these two particular kinds of shaping of the fingers in our further analyses of other Campin paintings.) The hands of Veronica in the X-rays lack the highly characteristic contour—a precision performance of the brush caused by the absence of white lead content in the critical gap. Their shape on the photograph is spongy and lacks crispness in the invisible lower layers. This technique suggests another, less exacting individuality than that of Campin.[5]

Now let us examine the blue sleeves. With side illumination we may recognize in a few spots impasto strokes making up a brocade pattern which is now concealed under the blue paint. In one spot the pattern is uncovered and reveals a black and yellow striation such as is used on the pattern of the gown to be seen at the bottom near the shoe. The sleeves, part of the brocade gown, were evidently covered up later by the uniform blue. This unexplainable alteration strangely coincides with the reworking of the sleeves of the London Madonna. Examination under magnification shows that the edge of the blue is underneath the adjacent flesh paint, thus establishing that the hands were painted only after the completion of the blue repainting. This is, I believe, an important discovery. The pictorial *matière* of the hands and the head is identical, and we may thus assume that their author is also responsible for the changing of the sleeves. The X-rays show chaotic and sketchy treatment of the area of olive-green fabric ruffled around the arm which considerably differs from the purposeful and precise brushwork of Campin. The very presence of this piece of drapery makes us dubious as to whether the entire sleeve area is by Campin for it is completely unrelated and illogical.

The head and hands of Veronica are so different in concept and execution from the usual typology of female faces and hands by Campin that a different artist is to be envisaged, who, nevertheless, attempted to conform fully with Campin's style. They are not alterations in the true sense, because X-rays do not reveal any differing *pentimenti*. It is likely that the master did not carry these areas beyond the preparatory drawing stage and the other man painted the unfinished area. This situation is also suggested in the Dijon Nativity and, to an even greater degree, in the left-hand wing of the Merode triptych.

The large fragment with the Bad Thief and two onlookers offers one an excellent opportunity to observe and to impress in one's memory the genuine, completely developed facial and character types found in the mature works of Robert Campin. There is an absolute consistency in all the elements of the design, the forms, the coloring and the brushwork. Only a few *pentimenti* can

5   Max J. Friedländer was suspicious of the hands: "Die Rechte mit der Veronika das Schweisstuch hält, ist nach allen Erfahrungen diesem Meister (i.e. Flémalle) nicht zuzutragen". (*Die altniederländische Malerei,* vol. II, Berlin, 1924, p. 69).

be discerned. One of them, the widening of the hair silhouette at the top of the crucified man's head, is a minor change. More interesting is the evidence revealed under raking light that Campin planned a narrow band across the crown of the head. Other minor changes concern the outline of his body.[6]

The condition of the painting is excellent like most of Campin's paintings, thus testifying to his sound craftmanship. However, the gold background shows signs of deterioration. It was formed by a stamped brocade pattern applied in large squares, but the design is considerably abraded.[7] A regilding has added to the confusion of the pattern and it is impossible to know today if color glazes were originally used to enrich the appearance.[8] The brocade is contemporary with the painting, as can be seen from the thick paint accumulated on the horizon line along the edge of the brocade leaf.[9] The addition of the hair mass is superimposed on the raised pattern, thus establishing that the brocade predates this change.

The artist's striving after a truthfulness of representation, formal precision and imaginative logic cannot be better documented than in the representation of the drapery about the loin of the thief. What appears to the casual observer to be an ordinary white loin-cloth, reveals itself on closer inspection, to be a carefully delineated long-sleeved shirt, complete with collar and seams stitched with bands of lace, and tied around the hips with one sleeve dangling. The loops and knots of the rope tying the thief's body to the cross convince us that this long rope was tied energetically and tightened so as not to be worked loose, tightened so much in fact that it cuts into the flesh of the man. One end of the rope, left dangling, is a most casual, original and unconventional representation and, as such, it had already been foreshadowed in the left-hand wing of Campin's early Entombment triptych.

The figures betray the sculptural feeling of the painter, this time in a work marking the *apogee* of his creative activity. His earlier plastic vision, as re-

6 The painter corrected the shape of the left leg by adding a small portion at the back of the knee and narrowing it just below the knee. It seems that the left hip was slightly larger in the underpainting, as flesh color shows through the adjacent gilding. The hand of the turbaned man which rests on the shoulder of the first man is less intensely realistic, and examination by means of X-ray radiation may perhaps help to determine its exact relationship to the rest of the painting.

7 In the wavy zones between scroll-like bands parakeet-like birds were perching on large stylized flowers. The bands were inscribed with illegible letters reminiscent of those on the brocade behind the standing Madonna.

8 The character of the damage to the raised brocade recalls the characteristic flaking of the resinous substance used for the relief brocade patterns on some fifteenth-century polychromed statues. It would be interesting to test whether it is a gesso paste or a rarer resinuous matter of the type mentioned above. Mojmir Frinta, "The Use of Wax for Appliqué Relief Brocade on Wooden Statuary", *Studies in Conservation*, vol. 8 (Nov. 1963), pp. 136-149.

9 The top of the spire of the tower is partly concealed by the new gold.

vealed in the Merode triptych, was a bold relief-like form. This primary concept evolved in Campin's later works to achieve an impression of statuary in
the round—their volumes most suggestively disposed in the space in daring
foreshortenings.

The solidity of the monumentally conceived shapes is logically expressed in
the very technique of rendering: the paint layer is rich, robust and applied energetically, and the forms are strongly outlined with a loaded pointed brush.[10] The
matière of the paint is not that array of free and spontaneous brushstrokes of
the later centuries which forms a haphazard relief, but is highly disciplined
and serves as a means of portraying the structure and texture of the objects.
We have seen it in the feathers of the angel's wings and on Joseph's cloak in
the Merode triptych and in the dabbing on the bottom of Mary's cloak on the
panel in Frankfort. The textures of the mailshirt, armor, jewelled brooch and
rope are rendered almost tactile. The short whiskers are painted in short impasto strokes. Another example of Campin's meticulous approach is the representation of the hair on the legs of the thief. Each individual hair was first
painted with thick white paint, observable as a low-relief in the side light, and
then gone over with a thin half-dry stroke of black. This was indeed a laborious method and it shows how deeply the painter was concerned with a realistic, integral and analytic representation of every motif, be it the knot of a rope,
precious stones attached to heavy hems or simply body hair. The utmost rendering of the substance, structure and mechanism of things was obviously of
primary importance to the artist. The precision of the tiny architecture in the
depth of the landscape calls to the mind the vistas in the Merode and Salting
paintings, and the cool, sandy colors of the bare landscape and road recall the
landscape in the Dijon Nativity.

Though the Bad Thief was usually represented as grimacing and of repul-
sive physiognomy, the artist, warmly sympathetic toward anyone suffering,
portrayed him as a noble being in the majesty of death.[11] The nobility of
countenance and postures, achieved in unique conjunction with naturalistic
details, is, no doubt, a precious flower which only rarely blossoms. But are we
absolutely sure that it is the wicked thief? Are we justified in applying without
a thorough weighting of the evidence our iconographic yardstick which tells
us that the man on the cross on the left side of Christ is the bad thief, to the
work of a highly original and innovating mind? Is not another interpretation
possible? I submit that the same tradition might have been observed here,
based however on a different orientation of the composition. A crude copy of
the retable in Liverpool (which is perhaps to be taken *cum grano salis* as a
unity) might be interpreted as the Calvary seen from the rear as the intense

10   A flaked-off portion on the right edge of the thief's shirt lays bare the cooler
white underpainting.
11   Panofsky, *op. cit.,* p. 167.

feeling for veracity suggested this view to Campin. He might have rationalized that the only efficient way to rest the ladder on a T cross is from behind and developed thus the whole composition on the rear side of the cross with the ladder stretching diagonally forward. The very same concept of the descent of the body of Christ while the ladder is resting from behind is used in the Deposition in the Prado. As a result the man painted on the right wing might have been indeed the good thief.

Furthermore, it may be of considerable significance that the crucified man on the left wing of the Liverpool copy (and likewise on the drawing in the Fogg Art Museum) is the model (only reversed) for the man in the etching by the *Bandrollenmeister*, identified by an inscription as "Gesinas malus".[12] Likewise his struggling pose is more characteristic of the bad thief. In the etching, he is in the correct place at the right. This did not happen by a simple mirror reversal of the scene because the rest of the composition corresponds figure by figure with the Prado Deposition.

12 Hamburg, Kunsthalle. Th. Musper, *Untersuchungen zu Rogier van der Weyden und Jan van Eyck* (Stuttgart, 1948), fig. 45.

CHAPTER VI

Two Portraits of a Stout Man in Lugano and in Berlin

A small portrait of a stout man in the Gemäldegalerie, Staatliche Museen in Berlin-Dahlem was attributed to the Master of Flémalle. The situation became complicated when another version, remarkably close, was recently found.[1] It reached the collection of Baron Thyssen-Bornemisza in Lugano-Castagnola and the two portraits were exhibited side by side in 1961 at the National Gallery in London. Even upon their confrontation the opinion of the experts remained divided as to which one of them is the original. The decision is difficult indeed as each of the versions has merits of its own.

I believe that ultimately only a morphological examination, study of the painting methods and an appraising of the intensity of the execution can yield some data for the solving of the problem: original v. copy.

The Lugano painting is more damaged and has one reassuring feature, namely that the frame is an integral part of the painted panel as we already have seen in other instances. The paint is of the type we have learned to recognize as typical of Campin—that is a dense thickly applied matière of an enamel-like quality. A steel-bluish color effectively renders the shaved beard on the upper lip. On the other hand, the paint surface of the Berlin panel is unexcitingly even, dull and generally thin. All impasto accents are missing as

1   F. Winkler, "Das Bildnis des Robert de Masmines (?) vom Meister von Flémalle", *Berliner Museen, Berichte aus den ehem. Preussischen Kunstsammlungen*, N.F., 1957, pp. 37-41.

in a disinterested routine performance. The color of the complexion is pinkish and the cool tones of the modelling are lacking.

All details of the Lugano portrait are executed with an absolute understanding of their form, substance and function and the strokes are decisive and purposeful, all that resulting in an unequivocal expression. This results in the intensity of facial features which is certainly superior in the Lugano portrait, in its naturalistic preoccupation. We may compare the masterly rendering of the wrinkles on the forehead which catches the essence and mechanics of the wrinkles to an only approximately statement of the same detail in the Berlin version. The same goes for the complete expression of the form of the lips and the nose, an analytical grasping of the expansiveness of the flesh masses as revealed on the silhouette of the face.[2]

The X-ray pictures are also instructive to our problem. Already A. Burroughs who published the X-rays of the Berlin portrait was fully aware of their difference from those of other Campin's works.[3] The accents in dense paint are not governed by a desire to mold the volume of the head to its full stereoscopicity and give instead a confused picture of the head's relief. In some spots these strokes follow the outline of a form instead of expressing its bulk. In the Lugano painting they are clearly articulated, more so than on the X-rays of the paintings sofar discussed. The reason may be that the upper paint layers are less dense and thus obscure less the lower layers which establish the bulk of the head. This appearance is close to the X-rays of a woman's portrait discussed in the next chapter. The infra-red photograph of the Berlin version reveals an un-Campinesque thick line underdrawing, which deviates in the tracing of the ear from the final appearance.[4]

An intense interest in the realism and the thoroughness in expressing it, a characteristic painting technique and color predilection in the Lugano portrait are those typical of Campins' works.

The Berlin portrait reveals a quite different artistic personality. The intensity of vision in regard to the shapes is replaced here by a less personnal and more idealized concept of form. It is perhaps a more lucid but unexciting type of painting. The interest in the decorative quality can well be perceived in the pattern of the hair and in a more superficial anchoring of the eyes into the volume of the head. All these are the qualities of Roger van der Weyden's paintings as I shall demonstrate on the Deposition from the Cross in the Prado.

2   I am thankful for some of the observations to Herr Böhm, Chief restorer of the Gemäldegalerie in Berlin.

3   Burroughs, *Art Criticism* . . ., fig. 7.

4   A similar coarse underdrawing is visible through the paint around the ears, chin and nose of the donor in the Crucifixion triptych by van der Weyden in Vienna, Kunsthistorisches Museum (No. 416). We already know that it was used also for tracing the donor in the Merode triptych.

The fact that there exist two versions of a painting, one bearing the characteristics of Campin and serving as a model for the other which is akin to Roger's works, is important for us. For it gives still another evidence of a close association of the two masters who collaborated on a famous masterpiece which I shall analyze subsequently.

Hulin de Loo proposed in the thirties to identify the Berlin portrait with Robert de Masmines, a high official of the Burgundian dukes. This hypothesis received a support by the circumstances of the appearance of the second portrait. It was preserved in the castle of Ponthoz near Huy whose ancestral owners were related to the family de Masmines. If the proposal is correct then the Lugano portrait is the earliest Flemish portrait in existence because it would have to be from before 1430 when Robert de Masmines was killed in the battle at Bouvignes.

CHAPTER VII

Portrait of a Woman in London

The style of the portrait of a woman in the National Gallery in London is in such perfect accord with the works so far discussed that I accept without hesitation its attribution to Campin. One sees here the characteristic solidity of forms in the treatment of both body and garment. The feeling of robustness—and, at the same time, precision—is matched by the forceful and decisive brush-work. The way the wrinkles on the knuckles are strongly recorded can be paralleled in previously discussed Campin's paintings. The voluminosity of the head is brought to its utmost effect and pervades all forms—even to the spherical shape of the eyeballs, as we have seen on the Bad Thief.

The portrait belongs to Campin's mature period and may date from the same time as the Crucifixion fragment or perhaps slightly later. There is nothing archaic or hesitant about her face; the sharp ridge along her nose and the slightly slanting eyes are very probably particular features of the woman portrayed and are not due to any deficiency in the drawing and modelling.

The X-ray picture shows that the head-dress was originally sketched in a different form;[1] the X-ray evidence is very instructive, as it reveals character-

1 It encircled the face of the woman in a curve coming lower on the forehead and the temples and bulging out at the ear. Its silhouette was wider on the left but seems to have been much lower at the top, ending just above the two pins. The lower outline of the folds of the material was scratched in (as revealed by the X-rays) with a sharp instrument; so were the scribbles on the sleeve on the extreme right which followed sketchy lines done in paint containing white.

istics in the building-up of the face which differ from the preceding pictures. The X-ray pictures of earlier works showed a considerable softness, haziness and even "smudginess" in the delineation of the highlights and features, the results of a particular working method. Here the brushstrokes of lower layers containing white are spelled out with precision, unobstructed by any clouding by successive layers.[2] We may observe that the appearance of the X-ray image is much more similar to the final appearance under ordinary light than it is, for example, in the Merode retable. I think that this difference between the two paintings may be explained by the evolution of the master's technique. In the Merode we find an involved brushwork which gradually builds up the modelling by means of thin layers of paint, the amount of white increasing as the modelling progresses. In the London portrait there is a more straight-forward technique of highlighting in the lower layers with a subsequent softening of the value contrasts by glaze applications. This represents a practical and effective short-cut in the earnest but painstaking process of the realization of form.[3]

2   White was used in copious quantities on the head-dress instead of utilizing the white of the gesso ground to obtain the effect of white paint modified by semi-translucent shading. (The latter principle was used, for example, in the portrait of a lady in the same gallery by van der Weyden.) Furthermore, the white was used emphatically for marking the short transversal wrinkles on the knuckles, for the fur trimming of the mantle and for various distinct highlights (on the upper lip, at the corner of the mouth, on the chin, two on the nose, on the eyelids, on the iris and on the eyeball).

3   It may be that the preference acquired later by Campin for a paint of a different viscosity and consistency, due perhaps to a modification of the formula of the medium, has conceivably led to a simplification of the painting technique.

CHAPTER VIII

Portrait of a Man in London

The paintings discussed above are those which I accept without reservation as belonging to the oeuvre of Robert Campin. There are several others which are attributed to him. My attitude toward them ranges from a reserve to a suspicion which leads, in some cases, to complete rejection. I shall briefly expound my reasons for my specific attitude in each particular case.

It is convenient to start with the portrait of a man in the National Gallery which is listed as a companion piece to the woman's portrait just discussed. Both are exactly the same size and from their first discovery in the early part of the nineteenth century have been considered a pair by the same artist.[1] Both are excellent paintings and would seem to form an unquestionable pair. Yet the concept and execution do not coincide exactly. The modelling of the man's face seems to be more advanced and its realism more photographic. The shadows are more scattered and, I would say, perhaps more "accidental": the kind which would displace themselves as one moved around the sitter. The shadows on the woman's face are more strictly limited to an underlining and strengthening of the chief features and their transition is very subtle. In this way, the spherical quality of her face is emphasized, which endeavor is carried down to the least detail. On the man's portrait, looser and more arbitrary strokes are used which reveal the artist's lesser determination about the forms. The paint of the flesh is less enamel-like and appears to be thinner. We may appreciate

1 Davies, *op. cit.*, p. 50.

the differences by comparing the emphatic roundness of the white of her eyes with a less masterly and less intense treatment of the same area in his eyes.[2] A somewhat looser execution may be detected also in the more amorphous brushwork of the man's fur collar as compared with the crisply drawn hair of the fur on the woman's cuffs.

The differences in morphology of details may be corroborated by a study of the radiographs. The whites in the woman's face are used more tightly and strictly to attain a three-dimensional effect. They produce less of a sfumato appearance than on the radiographs discussed above. The distribution of whites on the man's face is different. They are used in the underpainting without any clear sense of plastic gradation in the highlighted areas. They are also applied in the less prominent areas of the volumes where the basic modelling of the face does not directly require it, such as around the mouth and in the eyes.

One technical detail is worthy of consideration, that is, the curious quality of the wide craquelure on the red turban. It suggests the shrinkage of the film due perhaps to the excess of the oily medium or the presence of a siccative in the medium. I have not met other instances of such craquelure in the works attributed to Campin.

It is highly unlikely that one and the same artist would have used two painting methods at the same time for the execution of a pair of portraits.[3] The style, realism and lighting of the face seem to be more advanced on the man, and yet there is less resoluteness and contrasting pattern of light and shade in the picture as a whole. If they are really contemporary, then I feel that the author of the man's portrait belonged to a van Eyckian formation. The possibility that this is an early sixteenth-century copy, faithful to the original, cannot be excluded.

2   *Ibid.,* Pls. CXVII, CXVIII.

3   The scale of the man's head is somewhat larger, which may or may not give rise to some doubt as to whether the portraits were originally a pair. In any case, the identical size of the panel does not constitute a conclusive factor in the attribution, because a subsequently painted complementary portrait may have easily followed the same format.

CHAPTER IX

The Betrothal in Madrid

The panel with the Miracle of the Rod and the Betrothal of the Virgin in the Prado in Madrid is generally regarded as an early work of Campin. And indeed many features appear archaic—in particular, the composition, perspective and *coloris*. The surface is evenly divided into two scences and the wide caesura of the masonry forms a massive obstacle to the fluidity of the composition. This principle of a central division may well be a distant reminiscence of the manner of vertical partitioning of the panels in the earlier altarpieces, such as the Broederlam's wings in Dijon where the walls of the oratory and temple fulfilled the role of partitioning the wing.[1]

The general character of the Betrothal panel seems to indicate that it followed the Seilern triptych and preceded the Dijon Nativity. However, there are certain qualities almost too elusive to be described—in the perspective, figures and *coloris*—which make it difficult to recognize here the very spirit and creative personality of Campin. Though a few figures, such as the woman seen from the back with her mantle studded with gems on its border, and the

1 A similar principle is used to juxtapose two scenes in that astonishing work of art, the Tiefenbronn altarpiece from 1431 by Lukas Moser. His art is in some mysterious way connected with the blossoming of "magic realism" in the Low Countries, being in fact mainly associated with the art of Campin. A variation of this double scene was painted in the left part of a predella (?) panel in St. Catherine's in Hoogstraeten. It appears that Campin also used elsewhere the device of architectural elements to form a partition. It is used to separate the angel and Mary in the Annunciation in the Prado. This panel is a workshop replica, probably quite faithful in many parts, of a Campin work.

habit of Hebrew inscriptions on some garments, recall analogous figures in the early Campin's paintings, most of them are crowded into a compact mass without regard for their own space-occupying volumes, and no attention is paid to the explicitness of forms.[2] This I believe to be contradictory to the fundamental interest of Campin in material and plastic representation. The forms lack the breadth of monumentality and there is a considerable insistence on minute detail. The pattern, different on each of the eight columns supporting the cupola of the octagon in the Miracle of the Rod, is a pedestrian and pedantic *tour de force* and, because of its lack of subtlety and sense of proportion, is a distractive element. The execution of the architecture and the people is minute and too smooth and "tamely" groomed for the boldness of Campin's brushwork in the Seilern, Merode and Dijon panels.[3] The architecture is expertly designed and parts (i.e. the radiating buttresses in the foreground) show true understanding of the perspective; the profiling evident across the barely started splay of the left-hand portal corresponds exactly to the sequence of colonettes and mouldings on the finished right-hand portal. Yet the architecture as a whole is bizarre and nonsensical.[4]

There is a similarly unexplainable contrast between the accomplished aerial perspective of the distant landscape by means of degradation of color values and the realistically rendered clouds, on the one hand, and the aimlessly drooping portions of the landscape, on the other. A consistent horizon does not exist and the portions merely fill in the gaps in the architecture and the opening of the doorway.

The color harmony is distinguished by an array of gay, pure colors which bring to mind a bouquet of wild flowers. The pleasant gamut of primary and secondary colors may be a heritage of the conventions of the International Style, and it betrays the schooling and taste of a miniature painter. There is almost nothing of the earthiness of colors prevailing in the landscape of the

2   For example, a man only barely visible behind the buttress of the doorway manifestly occupies no space and is utterly unlike those ample and expansive forms in which all overlapping was reduced to a minimum.

3   Nevertheless, the impasto white on the shaved hair on Joseph's head may well be compared with Campin's characteristic tactile form of representation. Furthermore, an interest in realistic detail which conformed with the spirit of Campin's work may be seen in the hair-styles, the dresses, the individualized flowers silhouetted against the masonry and in such naturalistic details as the iron cramps in the blocks of the left portal and a straw mat, weighted down by a piece of wood and a rock, protecting the unfinished base of the portal.

4   The two portals are set obliquely to a narrow intermediary joining wall which is pierced by a window which has been barely started, while the massive round buttress at the right-hand end seems to suggest a stairway tower. Though the rear part of the octagonally domed structure may be interpreted as an apse, its front part loses its *raison d'être*, since one column is impossibly grafted on to the base of the left portal splay.

Dijon Nativity, and only a few colors of the generally more severe harmony of the Seilern Entombment may be compared.

The assumption can scarcely be denied that every great artist creates his own vision of humanity, a particular race of his own. However, it is possible that the artist in the course of his evolution rejects his earlier types and replaces them by new ones which more faithfully mirror his new concept of man and his ideal of beauty. Yet I believe that certain basic characteristics are always retained as a refrain throughout his creative work. It should be noted that neither Mary nor Joseph in this panel are the types which are portrayed either in early or mature Campin paintings. Instead, Mary with her precious lace-like crown is borrowed from the paintings of Van Eyck and is quite close to the Virgin in the Church in Berlin and to Mary in the Deësis and the Virgin Saints in the Ghent altarpiece. This would indicate that the author of the panel was influenced by van Eyck's art. There is a considerable amount of grimacing about the figures which can hardly be paralleled in any Campin picture.

The grisaille figures of St. James and St. Clara on the reverse of the panel are plastically weaker than the Trinity in Frankfort.[5] The style of the drapery, which is softer and without straight angular folds, is also different. The mechanical hatching on the fingers of James, apparent on the X-ray photograph, can be paralleled nowhere in Campin's works. The fingers are not representative of Campin but are rather like the additions in the Seilern and Dijon pictures.

To my mind, the Betrothal panel occupies an ambiguous position in the evolution of Campin's art, because it contains both archaic elements and elements symptomatic of a more advanced viewpoint. Of course, the presumably

5   The figures are placed in rectangular niches similar to those on the exterior of the wings of the copy of Campin's Deposition triptych in Liverpool. There is an uncertainty about the original function of the panel. If it were merely a part of a wing, as has been suggested, the outer face of the complete wing would have been painted with four figures in two registers somewhat like the interior of a Mosan triptych in the van Beuningen Collection in Vierhouten from ca. 1415 (Panofsky, *op. cit.,* Figs. 106 and 107). If this really is the earliest instance of figures in *grisaille* on retable wings, we must expect that the compositional scheme still probably will be in the experimentation stage, the esthetically most satisfactory solution not yet having been reached. The pose of a man clad in fifteenth-century dress on the extreme left who, looking to the side, appears to be disinterested in the scene may possibly be interpreted as that of a donor. Incidentally, he bears some resemblance to the donor in the Seilern triptych. His position at the very edge and gazing out to the left would acquire meaning if it could be assumed that the panel was the right shutter. The horizontally oblong shape of the panel suggests, that it was a shutter of a reliquary predella or one containing sculpture. The following examples of closing predellas may be cited: the shrine from Wiener Neustadt in St. Stephen's in Vienna, the Deocarus shrine in St. Lawrence's in Nuremberg, the retable in Kreglingen and the retable in Guttenstetten near Neustadt a. Aisch (*Zeitschrift des deutschen Vereins,* 1938, p. 125).

youthful works of any painter are much more difficult to estimate, since the style and technique are still uncertain and the artist has not yet mastered the equilibrium between his visual ideals and their means of execution. Though the evidence, some tallying and some conflicting with Campin's work does not lead to any categorically conclusive decision, nevertheless, it lays bare some puzzling inconsistencies. I believe I can recognize here, however, a much stronger miniaturist strain in the treatment of forms and colors than I could conceive of in a genuine work of Campin, no matter how early or late.[6] I feel that the painting, rather than being a youthful work of Campin, is a mature work of an eclectically oriented artist who must have been closely related to Campin and perhaps freely copied his composition. In any case, it could not have been a mechanical copy, since there are a number of *pentimenti*, such as the changing of the tassel of the apex of the high priest's hat. Significant for this painter is the tendency to crowd in more and more figures during the work, a true *horror vacui* pervading the whole. X-rays show that the head of a man to the right of Joseph was added (the architecture extends beyond).

6   K. Bauch (*op. cit.*) also voiced his doubts about the ". . . bunte Komposition aber ohne seine gespannte, spröde Eigenart in der Handschrift—wohl stets Kopie"—and further: ". . . hinter der Transzene Köpfe die einzeln betrachtet von Rogier sein (könnten)." The gay and overall "flowering carpet" gamut seems to be no anachronism in miniatures as late as 1460. *Vide* the Martyrdom of St. Andrew by the "maître du Mansel" (Valenciennes) in: *La fleur des histoires,* Fol. 9 in the Bibl. Royale, Brussels, Ms. 9232. *Le siècle d'or de la miniature flamande. Le mécénat de Philippe le Bon,* Brussels, 1959, color plate 2. Many excellent observations, coinciding with mine, were made by Lilli Fischer, "Die 'Vermählung Mariä des Prado zu Madrid," *Bulletin des Musées Royaux des Beaux-Arts,* Mars 1958, pp. 3-17. They point to the same negative conclusion as to the attribution to Campin.

A new, unorthodox, perspective may be gained by the recognition that archaic-looking paintings do not have to be necessarily early works. See the proposition of F. Lyna to date the panel of the Marys at the Tomb from the Beuningen Collection (previously ascribed to Jan van Eyck) to the late XV century (Frédéric Lyna, "L'œuvre présumée de Jean van Eyck et son influence sur la miniature flamande," *Sriptorium* XVI, 1962, p. 93 f.).

The Betrothal panel is similar in some respects to a Crucifixion in Berlin-Dahlem (No. 538A). Certain pedantism and archaic features appearing along with more advanced point of view perhaps reveal a late imitator of Campin's style.

CHAPTER X

The Trinity and the Virgin and Child in Leningrad
The Virgin in a Glory in Aix-en-Provence

I am in agreement with previous research, in the opinion that the three little paintings, namely the Trinity and the Virgin and Child in the Hermitage in Leningrad and the Virgin in Glory in the Musée Granet in Aix-en-Provence, belong to one style, but I am not sure that this phase could be convincingly fitted into the evolution of Campin's art. The people and their surroundings in the Leningrad pictures have an archaic flavor about them which disappears in the more svelte figures and more spatial setting of the Aix panel; yet, otherwise, they have much in common stylistically.

The two panels in the Hermitage are of identical size, and it has been established that they originally formed a small diptych. Their frames were carved in one piece with the panel like the Seilern wings but their profile was leveled off at a later time and painted with an ornament in gold and red.[1] The Trinity which was the left-hand half of the diptych looks more archaic than the interior with the Madonna seated on two pillows near the fireplace. The decisively painted faces of God and Christ are related to the Seilern figures, but the anatomy of Christ's body seems more evolved. The drapery style of

---

1 The panels measure 34, x 24,5 cm and the painted surface only 28,5 x 18,5 cm, Their backs are painted with a simulated marble pattern. They reached the Hermitage in 1845 and Ambassador D. P. Tatičev probably acquired them in Spain. I. Mikulin, "O pĕrvonačalnom vide Madony s mladĕncem i Troicy Flemalskogo Mastera", *Soobščenija Gosudarstvennogo Ermitaža* (Leningrad, 1958), pp. 32-34.

God's robe is similar to the figures in *grisaille* on the back of the Prado Betrothal. Both his mantle and that of Mary in the companion panel reveal under the infra-red light a tight underdrawing which, especially to the left of Christ's legs, recalls the astonishing underdrawing in the Merode triptych.[2] The strong modelling of the flesh parts in a red-brown gray can be well compared with that of Joseph in the Merode triptych. Analogy exists also in the impasto texture of the green tiles in the Leningrad and Merode interiors. However, the yellows and browns of the wooden objects are more reddish than the cool tones of the Merode. The great feeling for the quality of the material, its pliability or rigidity, its ponderation—essential to Campin—does not find here full expression. Neither is the effort necessary to keep the body of Christ upright to the side of God the Father's lap adequately portrayed: the recording of this phenomenon would have been doubtlessly of the utmost concern to Campin's realistic endeavor. Nor is the light logically represented: the semi-circular dais is unnecessarily darkened near the base of the throne, so that the sensation of the throne resting on it is lost. All this points to the early stage of Campin's development.

*

The domestic setting of the Virgin and Child scene closely resembles Campin's innovations in the Merode and London pictures. Several details from this painting may be met with in his other works.[3] Nevertheless, the style of the drapery, more arbitrary and superficially conceived, is unlike that in the Merode and London paintings. The ridges of the crumpled folds on the robe are too high and narrow and compose a serpentine and staccato rhythm unknown in the works hitherto discussed.[4] A notorious robustness of forms is here conspicuously absent. It should be noted that the types of Mary and the

2   The beard of God seems to have been extended subsequently. I have not seen the paintings and consequently, my observations, based on the photographic documentation, are only tentative. The Trinity in Louvain gives, according to my interpretation of Campin's evolution, a truer image of his style nearing its maturity. I shall discuss the latter in the Appendix where I deal with the copies and replicas.

3   E.g., the three legged stool in the same steep perspective and simple tile floor also exists in the London Madonna; its peculiar impasto rendering coincides with that in the Merode Annunciation; the pattern of the fur lining of the robe may be seen on the donor's wife in the Merode; the geometric pattern of squares grooved alternately vertically and horizontally on the row of tiles in front of the fireplace recurs in a variation around the fireplace of the Werl Barbara and is used, unchanged, as a border decoration of the collar and sleeves of Salome in Dijon and the centurion in Frankfort.

4   Some similarity may be seen in the treatment of the pillow in London but in Leningrad this has become exaggerated.

Child occur neither in early nor in mature works manifestly by Campin but are akin to the physiognomies of Jacques Daret's figures. Both faces and hands are weaker and duller, especially the Virgin's left hand which is unlike the energetic and structural hands by Campin. By the same token, Christ's left hand on the other panel resembles that in the Seilern Entombment, which I consider not to be consistent with the rest.

The elevated perspective viewpoint is similar to that utilized in the Merode but not to that in the London Madonna. It differs from Campin's space representation, as I understand it, in that the houses seen through the window are quite large and thus more true of a vista across a typically narrow street in a medieval Flemish town. On the other hand, the houses seen through the Merode and London windows are viewed as if through reversed opera-glasses and form a narrative microcosmos of their own. These two approaches are definitely different. The one used in the Leningrad panel is empirically a more advanced one, and yet it is inconsistent with the archaic perspective of the stool.

The X-ray photographs show the general characteristics of the Campin style (as does also the Betrothal panel), especially in the tracting of architecture and furniture; lighted shapes are neatly delineated with a thin brushstroke loaded with white. The body of Christ conforms, except for a looser treatment of the feet, to Campin's principle of modelling. More marked differences exist in the Madonna panel. The figures of Mary and the Child appear more vague and the brushstrokes are less determined and purposeful. Neither head is properly modelled and betrays a basic weakness in the concept of facial structure.

There is more vacillation and incertitude about forms and concepts in the Virgin's panel than in the Trinity. The vacillation between two viewpoints of space representation is more typical of a less original mind which lacks a convinced and highly personal vision of the world. There is nothing in the Trinity which would contradict the assumption that it is an early work as the stern character of some forms suggests. The baffling inconsistencies in the diptych may possible be explained by the hypothesis that the Trinity is a faithful reduction of an early Campin's composition, whereas the same collaborator took a few liberties in arranging the Campinesque scene of an interior with the Madonna, so that this panel is the weaker of the two. In any case, the diptych cannot be assigned to Campin's mature period because it lacks the creative principles and forms which he brought to full development.[5]

*

5 An attempt to date it was made on the basis of the Eyckian motif of basin-and-pitcher, considered to be a borrowing from the Ince Hall Madonna (1433); Panofsky, *op. cit.*, p. 172.

Striking resemblances exist in the faces of Mary in the panels in Leningrad and in Aix-en-Provence. Their expression and proportions are identical and the way the hair is combed is the same. The body structure in the latter painting is even more minute; her neck is slender and her hands with attenuated fingers are extremely delicate. This feeling of fragility and thinness of bone and skull structure, also characteristic of the other figures in this painting as well, is entirely alien to the robust and broad handling of Campin.[6] The head of Peter who is enthroned at the left recalls the cautiously painted heads in the Prado Betrothal. The style of the crumpled drapery in the Aix and Leningrad pictures is also convincingly similar (suffice it to compare St. Augustine's mantle with the Virgin's robe in Leningrad). The well painted landscape has a luminous quality but the vegetation is less intensely realistic and ebullient than in the Frankfort panels.[7]

The *coloris* of the painting enhances its quality as it uses a full orchestration of a wide range of colors. The coloristic sense of the painter is remarkable especially in SS. Peter and Augustine where a variety of colors compete one with the other in an overabundance. This is unlike the more restrained choice, yet forceful impression of Campin's colors which refuses any fragmentation. The dense ultramarine blue of Mary's mantle is like that in Leningrad and likewise her black shoe with a touch of red along the sole is painted identically in the two pictures.

The X-ray examination shows a certain quality of meagreness and dryness. White is sparsely used to build up the relief of the landscape with merely a few accents placed on the road, water and city walls. The pages of the open book are marked by sharp strokes of white along the edges without that soft transition from the highlight which distinguishes the very same detail in the Merode Annunciation. On the other hand, the clouds are crudely underpainted.

If we were to accept the characterization of Campin's art as inspired essentially by down-to-earth, bourgeois and realistic representational ideals, flavored by his insistence on everyday iconographical details, then the scene of the Madonna in Glory would completely belie this concept. Of course, the lofty scene could have been the commissioner's specific wish, which the painter had to

6 The face of St. Peter is unfortunately heavily damaged. The frame is most likely the original one and the coat of arms painted on the frame's bottom center may be related to the donor, an Augustinian abbot (*infulatus*) who is represented kneeling between the enthroned Peter and Augustine. Blue of the blazon's field and gold and red checks with dotted rosettes on the diagonal band show through the overpaint. On the back of the walnut (or oak?) panel there is an inscription carved with a knife: Leonardo da Vinci 1497.

7 E. Renders, *op. cit.*, Pl. 8C. The mode of the conventional grass painted with curved parallel strokes is that in the Seated Virgin in Berlin and in the donor's wing of the Merode retable.

follow, and the supernatural ingredient might not have been his choice at all. Yet there is much which is conventional and traditional in the scene, such as the decoratively arranged crown of clouds around the enthroned Madonna and Peter's large keys; one would expect some ingeniously devised transposition of this attribute to the level of everyday language. Notwithstanding the difficulty caused by comparing forms painted on a widely divergent scale, I find it strenuous to include these three little paintings within Campin's mature development. I prefer to consider them rather as eclectic works of high quality. I feel that the Leningrad and Aix panels are by the same artist. The Aix Madonna with Saints is more advanced and of an outstanding quality showing that the painter was at that time a fully mature artist. He may perhaps be identical with the author of the donors' wing of the Merode triptych.

*

The small panel with a Madonna on a Grassy Bench in the museum in Berlin-Dahlem belongs to the intimate circle of Campin's art but is generally not considered to be his own work. A strong archaic quality puts it into the beginnings of the evolution line, somewhere in the vicinity of the Seilern triptych. Yet the color is unlike the fine and original harmonies of the triptych. Here a heavy and traditional *coloris* points to a less exceptional artist. The flesh is of a warm rosy color and lacks the cool shading. The features are drawn in undecisive strokes.

The type of Mary appears to be close to the one in the free replica of the Merode Annunciation in Brussels. The formal treatment of the head recalls the two angels who do not fully conform in style to the rest of the Seilern triptych.[8] A formalistic and only superficial interest in veracity may be sensed in the Berlin picture in all details, be it the expressionless face, as if cut out along the hairline, or the vegetation of the mansonry wall. The handling of the grass falls short of the intense, realistic interest of Campin which is already seen to be far better in his early Seilern triptych and which is bound to arrive at mastery in his mature works. Though the painter tried here to introduce a variety of flowers, they, nevertheless, remain schematic; the grass blades painted with repetitive parallel strokes are monotonous without any "parti pris". The painting can be interpreted as essentially the work of a thoughtless

---

8   The conformation and expression of the eyes recall the German types, such as the Virgin in the Paradise Garden in the Staedel Institut at Frankfort. A certain parallelism may also be seen in the feminine types of Master Francke. Golden rays which radiate from the upper two corners and, at the same time, suggest a creasing of the back-drop fabric are a *retardataire* feature. M. Meiss also rejected the attribution to Campin. "A New French Primitive", *The Burlington Magazine*, June 1960, pp. 233-240. The Berlin Museum ascribes it to a follower of the Master of Flémalle.

imitator who did not bother to observe reality. Disinterested in the structure of things, he painted a stone (the wall really has neither stone nor brick quality) in the left-hand corner cut to an utterly impossible shape. The corner of a stone wall is never made by hewing large rectangular notches into blocks.

I consider this panel to be by an early assistant of Campin, the one who painted several figures in the Seilern triptych (J. Daret?).

CHAPTER XI

The Werl Panels in Madrid

I believe that special attention should be given to scrutiny of the two wing panels in the Prado—known as the Werl panels because the donor of the retable was identified by the inscription on the bottom left-hand wing as Henricus Werl from Cologne—for this is the only work in the entire group of paintings attributed to Campin which is firmly dated by the inscription as 1438, and the implication of its attribution to Robert Campin is immense in terms of the reconstruction of his artistic evolution and his personality. To recognize these two paintings, which represent the kneeling donor being presented by his patron saint, John the Baptist, and a seated St. Barbara in a domestic bourgeois interior, as Campin's implies that a peculiar twist has taken place in his later career. The obvious eclecticism in the two scenes is explained by the theory that Campin had exhausted his imaginative powers and artistic stimuli and was only able to keep pace with the achievements of the younger generation as epitomized by Roger van der Weyden at the price of being influenced by them.[1]

1 Panofsky, *op. cit.*, p. 174: "He could not step out of the circle which his own genius had drawn, and we can easily conceive that in the end he came to depend on those whom he helped to form."—Hermann Beenken, *Rogier van der Weyden* (Munich, 1951), pp. 20, 24, 26: "... In seiner Spätzeit steht er, so scheint es, ausser unter eyckischem, vor allem unter rogierischem Einfluss."—"Er ... verstand von den jüngeren Meistern zu lernen, weil er bis in sein hohes Alter auf die erstaunlichste Weise für Neues empfänglich war."—Alan Burroughs, *Art Criticism from a Laboratory* (Boston, 1938), p. 216: "Campin ... was an independent artist up to about 1438 when he recognized the strong talents of Roger and learned new lessons in grandeur ..."

As evidence for this hypothesis an illogical gesture of John the Baptist was cited, the model for which was rightly recognized in its functional representation in van der Weyden's panel from the Granada retable (The Metropolitan Museum of Art). There Christ appearing to Mary raises his right hand and shows the wound. The argument has it that Campin took this motif from a painting of his pupil Roger. This is not only an unflattering appraisal of the potentiality of a great artist, besides being unfounded, but, I believe, also one which lacks psychological insight and probability. Is it possible that the man who had enriched art by a vast gallery of new types, postures and, in fact, completely new pictorial concepts which were imitated for their sheer expressive power by many painters would now in his later years forsake and forget the richness of the creations residing in his mind and probably recorded in his sketches and stoop to borrowing a gesture which, moreover, has no meaning in this scene? What a sad picture of debased senility! In addition, he supposedly felt a need to borrow motifs from the Eyckian inventory: the round convex mirror on the wall is unquestionable an invention of Jan van Eyck as is also the inscription hewn in the stone slab painted at the bottom (it was then used by Jan's continuator, Petrus Christus).[2] It is interesting to speculate as to why the Eyckian influence would appear in the late phase of Campin's art, when, previously, the influences seem to have been in the reverse direction.[3]

On what grounds were these two paintings attributed to Campin? Are they unquestionably by him?[4] Are then these far-reaching conclusions about the decay of his artistic personality really justified? Barbara's room and the donor watching through the open door have been compared with the Merode triptych. These similarities, in fact, no more convincingly denote a common authorship than do the dissimilarities pointed out between some motifs in the Werl wings and some in the Rogerian Annunciation in the Louvre denote their divergent inspiration. (The rendering of two identical pitchers has been contrasted.)

One should be wary of attributing an identical hand to two paintings on the basis of similar iconography, similar specific details and similar types. It is, above all, the spirit and specific character of the execution that reveal the creator.[5] The question of quality, when viewed in a proper perspective and

2 This does not dispute the fact that there is a mutual fertilizing of artistic ideas among artists.

3 Ch. de Tolnay, *Le Maître de Flémalle et les frères Van Eyck* (Brussels, 1939), p. 24.

4 Paul Jamot, in his article in the *Gazette des Beaux-Arts*, 1928, p. 272, asked why the panels could not be by Roger, since it is precisely in such a man that we can expect an evolution toward a certain sweetness and gentleness. Furthermore, John the Baptist here is akin to John in the Bracque triptych by Roger (Louvre).

5 The differences of seemingly identical forms, easily detectable by a trained and sensitive eye, refute the "unitarian" theory of Emile Renders concerning Campin-van der Weyden.

context, has a weighty bearing, I believe, on the attribution.[6] Of course, in certain conditions of physical or mental deterioration, an artist's work may gradually (abruptly, in rare instances) lose its quality, but then the decline will probably affect all aspects of the work of art—powers of imagination, composition, invention, logic, psychological intensity—not just the actual draftmanship. In the case of these panels, the deterioration in quality has not affected all the components. For example, the mental tour-de-force of a charade which identifies the reading woman on the right-hand wing as St. Barbara by showing a tiny scene of a tower being built testifies to the intricacies of the author's mental faculties.

Both panels are fine paintings; the execution is refined, but the representation of some forms, mainly on the left-hand wing, lacks powerful, persuasive and bold authority. The bare legs of John the Baptist may serve as an illustration. According to art-historical research, the Werl panels certainly come almost a decade after the fragment with the Thief on the Cross in Frankfort. The scale is different in the two, but not to such a degree as to make the comparison impossible. In the Thief, there is a commanding knowledge of muscular and bony structure deliberately rendered in an expressive form, while, in John, there is an air of the uncertain and the approximate, without any conviction about the essential anatomy. In contrast to the individualization and specificness of the former, there is in John's leg a generalization which leads to an inexpressive form. The area of the ankle is vaguely smoothed down and lacks any relief characterization. The outline of the calf and the knee lacks any specific structural form.[7] It is truly inconceivable that an artist would forget his mastery of anatomical details, once he had acquired it. A cursory and careless rendering due to external conditions such as haste would, in actual fact, be detectable throughout the entire composition. It is rather the product of an imitator, in this case not without his own merit, who, in certain respects, attains the highest level, while, in other respects, he conceals under a slick and careful execution a lack of knowledge of true and vivid form. We search in vain for robustness and monumentality in every detail of the left-hand wing, be it the slender beams of the ceiling, the dwarfed steps or the insufficient thickness of the wall, but a gentle, subdued spirit of mediocrity has taken over the scene.

The right-hand wing with St. Barbara contains more characteristics of Campin's style than the left-hand wing with the donor. The forms are more robust

6   I cannot agree with Hugo von Tschudi when he says: "Die Qualität bietet für Zuschreibungen keinen zweifellosen Anhalt." ("Der Meister von Flémalle," *Jahrbuch der königlichen preussischen Kunstsammlungen*, 1898, p. 103).

7   The hands and bare leg of John, less confidently executed than in the Frankfort fragment, led A. Burroughs to make a significant though erroneous surmise that the Werl panels preceded the Frankfort painting. *Art Criticism from a Laboratory*, p. 214.

and the interior is more logically organized than the bizarre conformation of the other interior where a partition blocks off the rear of the room and the bench crowded in obstructs the full opening of the door—if one applies logic to the spaces represented. Moreover, the painting is of a higher artistic quality and is in sound condition, whereas the left-hand wing appears to be considerably damaged in the center.

The back of the donor's wing was cradled, whilst the back of the other wing has its original surface preserved. Under several layers of various paint two incomplete circles traced in impasto lines, can be discerned, the larger one in the top center, the smaller to the left and lower. These shapes and their relative positions may be interpreted as haloes of a standing Virgin and Child.[8] Unfortunately, no X-ray pictures were made to corroborate the interpretation.

The style of Barbara's drapery, and even more of the donor, is related to the three little panels previously discussed, and the crinkly quality may have evolved from them. The colors in the left-hand wing are visually blended together without giving an impression of the self-contained, strong color areas such as we have seen in the Merode altarpiece. Even the pure colors of Barbara's dress (green, blue, gray, red and yellow brocade) and the red cloth on the bench are brought together without any of them being given any prominence. It may be argued that the harmonizing of color and the resulting less forceful coloristic effect could mark an artistic evolution. The stone floor in the left-hand wing has a pinkish hue unlike the cool grayish or sandy color in genuine Campin paintings. The tiles in the right-hand wing are alternately pink and yellow, which produces too sweet a harmony. The landscape seen through the window behind John the Baptist is dull, whereas the scene with the tower is superior to it in color and atmosphere. The choice of tones and tints for the flesh parts is different from the exemplary works of Campin, and is distinguished by a more rose-brown tonality and paint of coarser quality than the enamel-like cool ivory, translucent pink and tan colors of the master. The presence of these two sets of coloristic choices associated with two kinds of formal treatment was noted in the Dijon Nativity.

The notation of light and shade phenomena is vigorously followed through, especially in the interior with St. Barbara where the strong double-cast shadows

8   See also E. Renders, *op. cit.*, and Paul Pieper, "Zum Werl-Altar des Meisters von Flémalle", *Wallraf-Richartz Jahrbuch*, XVI, 1954, pp. 87-103. He deduced from the poorer condition of the donor's scene that this painting may conceivably have been the exterior face of the left-hand wing facing the Madonna, now overpainted, when the retable was closed. The interior of the wing might have had a Visitation as a pendant to the seated Barbara. The less ingenious assumption of other people that the paintings are those of the closed wings create the peculiar iconographical situation that a donor presented by his patron-saint would have reverently observed another saint.

are recorded with geometric precision. They are less distinct in the donor's panel, as the light seems to be softer there. The vigorous shadow of the brass pitcher is painted with such consummate skill that it recalls the rendering of the shadow cast by the laver in the Merode Annunciation. The light coming through the window and the competing light of the fire each create shadows of their own. Even prismatic color reflexes are caught within the shadow cast by the glass carafe on the mantlepiece. One over-zealous double shadow has crept on to the floor in the left-hand bottom corner, which has been cast by some unknown object beyond the edge of the scene. Its puzzling presence may be explained in two ways. On the one hand, it may be that the center and right-hand paintings formed one united interior,[9] and a piece of furniture (as the straight line of the shadow suggests) ought perhaps to be imagined at the right-hand bottom of the lost center panel. On the other hand—and more probably—it is perhaps a residuum, thoughtlessly reproduced, of a model Annunciation scene which has been adjusted to a new iconography. A jug of lilies standing on the floor in the center front casts a shadow in this very spot in a copy of a lost Campinesque original.[10]

9   *Ibid.*, p. 98.
10   A low vase with lilies, also casting a triangular shadow exists in an Annunciation by a Westphalian painter called the Master of Schöppingen (P. Pieper, *Meisterwerke der Gotischen Malerei Westfalens*, Pls. 16 and 17). This painting is a provincial imitation from the middle of the century of a composition by Campin (or inspired by him) of which a replica exists in the Musées Royaux in Brussels. (Carla Gottlieb, "The Brussels Version of the Merode Annunciation", *The Art Bulletin,* March 1957, pp. 53-59.) One may compare the position of the Virgin, the little broom hanging on the wall and the pouch on the floor. The wooden corbels supporting the beams of the ceiling in the Schöppingen picture seem to come from the Barbara wing rather than the Brussels replica, as there are stone corbels in the latter which are identical to the Merode original. However, the similarity of motifs may serve only to indicate a connection and is not relevant as to the authorship. They are easily transplantable and, in themselves, do not really constitute hallmarks of an artistic identity (viz. the towel hanging on the rack, the burning fire, the above-mentioned pattern of tiles in the Werl Barbara and the Leningrad Madonna, the glass carafe and brass in the Werl and the Louvre Annunciation and Jan van Eyck's paintings). I think that there are various indications to show that the Annunciation scene preserved in an associate's copy in Brussels was perhaps the basic and older composition and the Master's variant in the Merode triptych was a more exclusive and special version. In the first variant, provision was not made for the highly original iconography of the witnessing donor, as the door was painted further to the rear. This "standard" version became more famous and widespread as it was copied in various media. In addition to the Schöppingen panels, a bas-relief in Magdeburg (Th. Rousseau, *op. cit.,* p. 124) and a Bohemian panel from about 1460 (Jaroslav Pešina, *Painting of the Gothic and Renaissance Periods,* Prague, Pl. 15) may be mentioned. Some misunderstood forms and distortions of both may indicate that the scene was conceivably disseminated by means of a woodcut. The Merode composition exists in two copies — a faithful copy in Kassel (Burroughs, *Art Criticism* . . . Figs. 106 f.) and another in a private collection in Genoa (V. Denis, "Un nouvel argument en faveur de l'unité de

There is no doubt that the style of the right-hand wing is very close to Campin's style as it may be presumed to have evolved in his later years. The physiognomy of St. Barbara is close to his own types, as is shown by the massive neck, the proportions of the features and the treatment of the hair. The intense interest in the appearance of the shadows and the comprehensive perspective have been noted above. The left-hand wing is weaker in its execution, compositional clarity and morphology. The re-use of a gesture not in keeping with the countenance of St. John and conceivably of an amended iconographic scene emerges as a strange and eclectic working pattern in these two panels. If we accept the hypothesis of P. Pieper that the panel with the donor was really the outer face of the left-hand wing, then it becomes plausible that a collaborator was entrusted with its execution, as sometimes happened in the closing retables. Campin might have painted the interior faces of the triptych. One remaining possibility is that the retable was a contemporary pastiche but, nevertheless, quite a competent work. My reservation to its being attributed to Campin is primarily derived from my judgment of the donor's wing (and perhaps only from that). This qualifying opinion as a result does not destroy the image of Campin as an independent artist. Final judgment must be withheld until a more thorough documentation is available.

l'œuvre de Roger van der Weyden", *Annales de la Fédération Historique et Archéologique de Belgique*, 1953, pp. 541-7).

CHAPTER XII

The Reading Magdalen in London

The problems of attribution are well illustrated in a fragmentary panel in the National Gallery in London representing the Reading Magdalen. Something Campinesque and, at the same time, Rogerian led some critics to attribute it either to the one or to the other artist; and indeed the style of the painting seems to fall between the two attributions. To my mind, the painting is nearer to Campin than to van der Weyden but it is not necessarily by the former.[1] The case history of the panel as established by Norman Brommelle during the restoration of the painting in 1956 is interesting.[2] A dark uniform overpaint of the background was removed and a domestic interior with portions of two

1   I agree with Alan Burroughs' repudiation of Roger's authorship on the basis of the uncharacteristic brushwork on the face revealed by the X-rays. (*Metropolitan Museum Studies*, IV, p. 138, Fig. 8): "We are justified then in placing the Magdalen apart, as being not in agreement with Roger's early work". He saw a similarity between the shadowgraphs of the Magdalen and the Berlin Crucifixion and suggested the same author for both (p. 139). However, if we accept the theory of an extreme similarity between Roger's early style and that of his master it becomes conceivable that he collaborated to a large extent in the painting.

2   It was found that the panel had been re-used. A painting which had probably been discarded had been covered with another layer of gesso and the present painting executed upon it. In the first layer of gesso a very fine canvas was embedded; such a practice is without parallel in the group of Campin and van der Weyden panels. (Wood overlaid with canvas and gesso was a commonly used support in earlier Bohemian and German paintings.) The London fragment was transferred to a new mahogany support. The original size of the whole panel may be estimated to have been about 110 x 160 cm.

more figures was revealed. A bust of an old man in the Gulbenkian Collection in Lisbon was identified as the missing upper part of a saint standing on the right.[3]

The style of the painting and the physiognomy are connected with pictures associated with Campin's art. A face comparable to the Magdalen's is that of the Werl Barbara. Yet it seems that the face of the Durán Madonna (also in the Prado) attributed to Roger stems from the same prototype. The observation of H. Beenken on the stylistic proximity of a small standing John the Evangelist in the Berlin Museum to the Magdalen may suggest that both were painted by the same hand.[4] On the other hand, there is affinity between the man's head (St. Joseph?) in the Gulbenkian Collection fragment and the Portrait of a Man in Prayer in the Metropolitan Museum of Art.[5] Both the brushstrokes of the eyelids, wrinkles, and ear and the meagre and thin application of paint are analogous in both male heads and, to a certain degree, on the Magdalen picture (cf. the fur hems on the garments of the Magdalen and the Praying Man).

There seems to be no doubt that this panel was painted by someone intimately acquainted with Campin's art, perhaps even under his supervision, as is shown by a comparison of the representation of various elements with Campin's own rendering. There is the same desire for an emphatic plasticity, voluminousness and monumentality, as can be seen in the concept of the draperies, the jar of the ointment on the floor, etc. Yet their effect falls short because of the emptiness of the form and a non-organic exaggeration of its character. The folds ruffled on the male saint's sleeve are too many and too confusing; the scooped-out ends of the narrow deep folds stop abruptly without modulation and are painted more crudely and with less love for a perfected shape.

Despite the fact that the degree of realism is considerable, some details show less intensely observed forms which are so typical of Campin. The portion of the Magdalen's fur-lined upper garment, folded and pulled up on the knees, is a known motif, but it is painted here with less sensitivity and less observation of the actual appearance. It is a formalistic shape not studied from nature. The white protective cloth of the book is simply creased. The form, rather than being simplified by an effort toward clarity and monumentality, thus lacks interest. The nails on the board floor are too mechanically blunt, unlike the same detail in the carpenter's shop in the Merode wing which is rendered with a keen sense of the right measure of intensity. The wall, two seats in the recess of the window and its mullion are not painted with a concern for expressing

3   Reproduced in Friedländer, op. cit., II, Pl. XXXXIII, No. 36. On Pl. XXXXII a bust of Mary or an unknown saint is reproduced, said to be a fragment from the same panel. This is not possible because of the differing style and quality.

4   Beenken, op. cit., p. 31 and Fig. 14.

5   Panofsky, op. cit., Pl. 221 and Fig. 361. Ex Coll. Colnaghi.

the nature of their material, which we can only guess to be stone. The schematization of the knotty staff in the saint's hand is far removed from the sense of the individualized form of the beams in the Dijon Nativity. The panels of the cupboard are rendered with an effect of overall dullness and monotony. The fingernails and toenails and some of the fingers themselves are badly formed and smallish, as they are on the feet of John the Baptist in the Werl wing or on the shepherd's hand in the Dijon Nativity.

The vacillation between a superficial and insensitive treatment of some details and a painstaking and careful painting of other is similar to that in the painting of the donor's wing in the Merode triptych. The gold trimming on the end of the Magdalen's sash, the translucent beads of the rosary and the rendering of the brocade dress are miniature-like and consummate, as are the trimming on Inghelbrecht's purse and the tiny pendant worn by his lady. On the other hand, the stones studded in the hem of the Magdalen's dress are painted much more schematically than the beads. The hinges and lock on the cupboard are painted exactly like those on the door in the Merode wing.

The eclecticism of an assistant of Campin, or rather his pupil, may be perceived also in the domain of color. He was likewise striving for a strong impact of color as we know it in Campin's works (exemplary in the Merode and Frankfort panels). His colors too suggest a predominantly cool harmony but their number is exaggerated and the chromatic unity of the ensemble is thus impaired.

The juxtaposition of three strong primary colors on the standing figure, i.e. the azurite blue of the cloak, the red of the undergarment and the yellow of the lining, is perhaps too restless and aggressive, since their immediacy and compactness lack the soothing effect of the softer and less pronounced colors which would be expected to balance the area. Again the coloring of the figure of the Magdalen does not evoke the characteristic color juxtapositions of Campin.[6] Strong red consisting of vermilion with a top layer of crimson madder-like red colors the cloak of the kneeling saint. There is an array of reds, blues, whites and grays in the landscape. Our apprehension of the multiplicity of the color scheme is only partial, as our panel is just a fragment of a large painting. We must expect quite a strong color concentration in the lost

---

6 Her heavy garment is of a yellowish green with highlights in pale yellow. The pigments are lead white and litharge or massicot mixed with copper resinate. Unlike as in Campin's greens, here the top layer is not formed by transparent copper resinate glazes (from the report of Norman Brommelle at the National Gallery in London). The Magdalen's silk sash is of a dark indigo-like blue. The contrast is provided below in the red cushion on which she is seated. The odd dull yellow-brownish gray of the brocade gown has gold threads painted rather thinly in the same light yellow and shaded with umber. The lining is in a dull red, while the fur lining of the upper garment is in a Campinesque cool gray.

central group which probably contained a seated Madonna.[7] From what we have, there is an indication that the whole scene was a little too garish. The colors of the background have a quality different from the comparable areas in Campin's work. These areas are markedly tinted, unlike the truly neutral background colors of Campin. The plaster of the wall is darker and more bluish than a corresponding silvery shaded area of the wall in the Merode Annunciation. The wooden floor is more purplish gray than the absolute gray in Joseph's workshop. Campin probably added to the black and white a little umber, while the painter of the Magdalen panel perhaps used red iron oxide instead. This pigment constituted the brown of the cupboard, with an admixture of vermilion.[8] On the other hand, Campin's furniture shows more sandy shades of siennas and ochres, while his shutters are in cooler browns most probably containing some umber. The ivory color of the Magdalen's hands with gray shadows is well in keeping with Campin's preferences. However, the hands of Joseph (?) and feet of the kneeling John (?) have an orangy warm hue (vermilion and brown iron oxide) and are pale buff in the shadow.

The X-ray picture of the Magdalen's head shows the brushwork to be very close to early Campin paintings such as the Merode retable. The effect is slightly nebulous; no dense paint was applied in the cavities of the eyes and along the nose, exept on the ridge of the nose and the eyelids. There is a gap in the white film modelling the forehead just underneath the edge of the headgear, suggesting that the shadow was not painted over the light flesh paint. An economical purposefulness of means is thus borne out. The mouth seems to be somewhat smaller than in the final appearance. The modelling of the cheeks with white applied in soft, liquid, almost indistinguishable strokes, which extends continuously from the cheekbone to the mouth, recalls the face of the Madonna Suckling Child in Frankfort. The standard underpainting of the female faces by Roger consists, on the other hand, of a concentration of the white highlights on the middle of the cheeks. Likewise, the hands conform in their X-ray appearance with Campin's early use of delicate white touches.

The infra-red picture reveals an underdrawing with thick and coarse lines. The fingers are drawn in only approximate shape and, in general, do not correspond to the final tracing of forms. The nose was drawn bigger, the nostrils were more prominent and the line of the jaw was originally higher. The hori-

7   Martin Davies, "Rogier van der Weyden's Magdalen Reading", *Miscellanea Prof. Dr. D. Roggen* (Antwerp, 1957). This is inferred from the drawing in the National Museum in Stockholm by the Meister der Koburger Rundblätter (Fig. 4). One wonders if the little scene with the archer seen through the window is not another cryptic allusion to the donor's favorite saint, which would here be St. Sebastian, basing our inference on the case of the Werl Barbara. Such charades would then reveal the state of mind of the atelier.

8   This rather unusual addition was analytically established by Miss Joyce Plesters.

zontal lines on the cupboard were also considerably higher. This sketchy technique of cursory thick lines may well be compared with the infra-red evidence of the donor's wing in the Merode triptych.

The similarity to Campin in the underpainting of the face is puzzling and the possibility of his participation in the first stage of the painting of the Magdalen's head and hands cannot be entirely ruled out. The associate, who perhaps executed the work from the master's design was, however, so thoroughly imbued with the pictorial idioms of his master that only an inferior naturalistic feeling, an inferior sensitivity reflecting itself in an inferior quality and his own chromatic vision distinguish his style from that of Campin. The divergencies from Roger's mature style are greater, but we do not know how eclectic his early style would have been. The question as to whether it was early Roger or some other pupil must remain open.

In the same way, the classification of the portrait of a young lady with a large white headdress in Berlin-Dahlem (No. 545 D) as a work of van der Weyden is by no means assured. The volume is stressed to the maximum, all forms—the face, the eyes, the breasts, as well as the folds—are as if bulging under an inner pressure. This is typical of the stereometric concept of Campin, whereas the forms of van der Weyden are rendered more lineary and the expansive tension of their volume is deflated to a mere twodimensional calligraphic design.

The hands are the type favored by Campin: massive, almost stocky with marked knuckles. The nails are squarish and ending almost straight but they sink into the cuticle as they curve more than the fingers do. Van der Weyden's nails are flat, oblong and strongly curving at the top in a claw-like fashion. They are as if appended to the fingers rather than growing out of them. The hands in the Berlin picture are painted in a thick paint in cool greyish colors. Likewise the lights along the eyes are solidly painted. There is also the tactile quality of the heavy fabric conveyed by the characteristic technique of tiny impasto dabs on the ridges of the folds.

The contrasting approach is evident in the hands of a young Lady in the National Gallery in Washington, which are typically Rogerian. Their clasp is unpleasantly cramped and illogical as they produce a bulkless arabesque. It is difficult to see how both portraits could be attributed to the same artist.

CHAPTER XIII

The Descent from the Cross in Madrid

After the examination of the works attributed with more or less certainty to Campin has been completed, the climax of the present study is reached. It is the throwing of some light on what I believe is the secret of the Descent from the Cross from the Escorial (now Prado), titanic in its aloofness from the Roger van der Weyden's style. Upon an examination of the painting's surface I became convinced that two artistic individualities participated in the painting. My working method was to examine first the appearance and thickness of paint layers and brushstrokes in relation to the artist's own personal idiomatic painting habits, then the choice and qualities of color such as the density and lustre, and, finally, the specific chromatic flavor of secondary and tertiary color mixtures. Then I tested the results by comparing them critically with the form and expression. In the light of my findings, the whole composition can be divided into two groups of figures with only limited areas where both pictorial characteristics appear to be superposed.

The paint is rich, thick, unctuous, and, in places, almost impasto on the majority of the surface, while the remaining part is characterized by a thin, drier, even, and impersonal application of the paint. A massive layer of white paint, applied with a great feeling for relief and worked by a stick, models vigorously the kerchiefs of the swooning Virgin, the weeping woman on the left and the jacket of the youth on the ladder, but it is less noticeable on the sheet on which the body of Christ rests and on the kerchief of the Magdalen which is, nevertheless, very close in style to the other two kerchiefs. The creamy paint of the youth's hose is energetically applied in a solid layer and outlined in black. The pattern of his velvet jacket is rendered by the vigorous impasto strokes of white and faintly ice-bluish colors. It reveals a determined and intense concern for the complete textural expression of a material. Instructive of the difference between the two artistic personalities is the comparison of two velvet materials; the green one on the skirt of the young woman is delightfully tactile as a result of the variation of the paint thickness forming the pattern, whereas the red one on the Magdalen's sleeves lacks any paint relief. This difference has no effect on the artistic quality, as both representations of the similar large patterns are superbly painted.

The thinness of the paint "matière" exists throughout the figure of the Magdalen. The red tunic of Joseph of Arimathea is also painted in the same spirit: the brushstrokes are dry and meagre. However, the red of his hose is brushed on in the form of small thick paint drops, which effect approaches the robustness of the paint on the older woman, the Virgin and the youth. The appearance of the rendering of Joseph's tunic is to be compared to the red madder garment of John, which is painted with dashing, yet undecided and superficial brushstrokes; the paint is dry and thin. This quality can easily be appreciated by contrasting it with the dense and opaque grayish purple blue on the mantle of the woman on his left and the deep blue of the Virgin's mantle. In addition, both garments are conceived much more in terms of light and shade than on John's.

This sculptural feeling is heightened in the strongly lit areas of some faces and hands (mainly the Virgin's) by thick white paint in an *unisono* of material means and expression. The unctuous paint on Mary's neck and collar-bone, for instance, shows the dabbing imprints of the brush, and the wrinkles on the knuckles are worked with a stick. On the other hand, the painting of the wrinkles on the forehead of St. John, Joseph and the man on the right is thin, and the dark line is inseparably coupled with a light stroke running alongside; this manner oversimplifies the subtle light condition of the epiderm and stems basically from a linear, abstract and anti-naturalistic concept. How different from the highly plastic rendering of the furrows on Nicodemus' forehead! The paint on the latter head is more compact and involves a masterful handling of the color paste with the brush. The crystalline statement of the essence of the shape of the eyes which acquire an almost metallic quality may be compared with the crisp and precise treatment of the eyes in the female portrait by Campin in London and is in contrast to the less precise and more softly painted eyes of John. The expansive voluminosity of Nicodemus's head fails to be convincing on John's head which is rendered by rather timid and painstaking brushwork. The same can be said about Joseph's face and, furthermore, about that of Veronica in Frankfort. Likewise, the face of the young woman supporting Mary is painted with unemotional brushstrokes and the paint, unlike that on Mary, is thin and spread evenly, although the style of the mouth and nose is basically the same on both.

The duality in the paint application and its varied density, used as a means of illusionistic representation of the structure and details, may be perceived from an examination of the tears on the face of Mary, John and the young woman. Mary's tears are painted with a "loaded" brush in a solid form and the white reflection on them is so painted that it gives the illusion of transparency only from a distance. The bold and distinctly shaped reflection is similar to that recorded on the precious stones on the nimbus of Mary, on the centurion's brooch in the Frankfort panels, on the hem of Salome in the Dijon Nativity and on the hem of Joseph's red undergarment in the Descent. On the other hand, John's and the young woman's tears are brilliantly painted with thin and blended glazes and shine in a *trompe-l'œil* fashion but are without substance. The mastery of this more miniaturist approach can particularly be appreciated upon observation from close at hand and may well be compared with the technique of Christ Appearing to Mary (in the Metropolitan Museum of Art). This diversification in the rendering of details corresponds with the two types of color application and brushwork—robust and thin.

The effect of the glowing and saturated colors is sonorous and the gold adds to the solemnity and magnificence of the painting. The strong appeal of the colors is achieved by the concentration of each over a large area; but, within these areas, affiliated colors sparingly used enrich like stars the otherwise too strictly regimented chromatic distribution.[1] The color harmony of the right-hand part of the composition is less boldly virile and direct than in the center and left-hand parts. The color is generally lustrous and defines the shapes and textures with the utmost tangibility in their material substance. Yet in some restricted areas the color is lustreless and dull and lacks strong contrasts of values. Such an area is the left foot of Nicodemus: the paint lacks body and lustre and is slick and dull, as if seen through a filter which reduces the luminosity. Yet his other foot is painted energetically like Mary's hands, the skull or the grass on the left. The red of John's garment has a rich and complex tone vibrating with cooler and warmer hues in its lower part, but it becomes more dry and primary in the upper part.

The color treatment of the faces shows two distinct characteristics which are directly related to the variegated density and impasto of the paint film, and to its smoothness and thinness in other instances. The faces of Mary, the old

---

1   The refined color sense of a mature master may be seen at its best on the youth in the center. His long white jacket and the fluttering striated strip of his head-band are shaded with a subtle glacier-blue color reminiscent of the angel's robe in the Merode Annunciation. A fine variation is introduced by the creamy color of his hose. The accents of subdued brown and red and green in his vest are sensitively dosed in the midst of creamy and bluish whites so as not to offset the light character of the area.

woman, the youth on the ladder, Christ and Nicodemus are painted in cool harmonies with gray shadows. The color varies as the typological characterization requires it: the bloodless face of the swooning Mary and of the youth are grayish white and are the most moving portrayals of a grief ecstatic beyond bearing. The corpse of Christ has the yellowish waxiness of the dead. The faces of the weeping woman on the left and of Nicodemus have a livelier pink and a darker complexion, respectively, in accordance with the representational convention for older people and male types.

The remaining faces, i.e. John's, Joseph's, the young woman's, the Magdalen's and the man's behind Nicodemus are basically characterized by a light pink-brown which becomes bronzy-brown in the man on the right. The shadows are invariably warm with a strong content of reddish brown. The paint is less opaque and is thin. It seems to be less finely ground. The brushstrokes are less integrated into a fine gradual weave of modelling and fail thus to convey the highly sculptural volumes of the first group of heads. The accents are linear and the transitions are too abrupt, and they actually break the spherical shape of the head into a flattened and even anti-voluminous form (John).[2] It was precisely the lack of balance between the components of incisive drawing and rendering of volume, combined with an impure-looking coarse pinkish-brown paint, which was so characteristic of the head and hands of Veronica in Frankfort. Even at the level of psychological impact the parallel is maintained: these faces are much more worried than deeply grieving.

This exaggerated insistence on linear quality also pervades the face of Joseph. The pinkish upper layer of paint stops abruptly on the forehead just short of the edge of the skull-cap, thus leaving visible a narrow band of different paint which resembles the enamel-like quality of the first group of faces. This may lead to the supposition that this layer continued beneath the present face which would then possibly be an overpainted mask. The similar presence of two superposed color films differing in consistency and "personality" may also be seen on the left arm of Christ where the muscular structure is as if appended to the broad underlying shape and does not grow organically out of it. The lower layer here is likewise thick and dense while the overpainting strokes float on the top and do not consistently cover the entire form.[3]

Now let us evaluate the scene of the Deposition from the standpoint of correctness of action and gestures. First let us examine the relation of Nicodemus' foot, which we observed to be weakly painted, to his body. Its position is not

2   The construction of John's head may be compared with the first of the Magi in the Columba altarpiece in the Alte Pinakothek in Munich. Beenken, *op. cit.*, Fig. 101.

3   *Pentimenti* in the dangling end of Nicodemus' headgear and the collar area show changes in the design. The collar fur seems to have been added and the forehead was originally lower. Owing to the absence of documentation by means of penetrating rays photography, we may have missed possible changes in our examination of the surface.

only disturbingly ugly and impossibly twisted but contradicting the very spirit and logic of the scene.[4] The head and torso are a part of a powerful pillar-like stance which conveys an idea of a great solemnity and ceremonial slowness. Yet the feet suggest a walking and almost a dancing movement and their relative position can be explained only by a cross-legged posture. This motion is absolutely divorced from the rest of the body, since in the torso and waist there is no indication of the *contrapposto* which would be necessary to join the upper part, slightly turned to the left, to the walking motion emphatically directed to the right. The diagonal pull of the drapery could be taken as a not too happy reconciliation of the two disparate parts. The present stance is a precarious one, which is never assumed by a person just receiving a heavy burden in his arms. Furthermore, the cross-legged stance is a formalistic idea and —because of the implication it conveys of moving away—is incompatible with the stable and balanced position needed to receive Christ's body safely. Finally, the walking-away movement disturbs the very spirit of the patently centralized composition.

However, the boldly painted foot on the right, which, in the cross-legged posture, must be the right foot, could, in fact, be his left foot if we were to visualize Nicodemus' pose as a straight, braced-up stance of the heavy body. This interpretation would, of course, require a totally different pose of the other foot, which , in this case, would be his right foot. It would have to point to the left. The present hybrid pose could have come into existence because the other painter had misunderstood the secure stance of Joseph, taking his bending knees and separated legs for a walking movement, and had introduced it *per analogiam* into the unfinished figure of Nicodemus.[5] The foot on the left which upsets the logic of the pose is his work.

4   It is interesting to surmise that Michel Coxcie in his faithful copy of the painting must have felt the deficiency of the pose of the "left" foot and have made a minor change in the design which was, however, no improvement. He also took the liberty of putting the cross in front of the tracery, thus disregarding the principle of containing the scene within the space of the illusory shrine. Otherwise, he closely adhered to the original, so that only very minor changes affecting the precision of the folds and a slightly more raised little finger on Mary's left hand may be perceived. The countenances of the people, nevertheless, betray the copy; the faces lack the intense life of the original. It is, of course, very difficult to catch the identical psychological personalities in a reproduction work. It is perhaps an unintended tribute to the accuracy of the copy which is now in the Escorial that it has been reproduced as the original in several recent scholarly publications.

5   The idea of a walking movement exists, on the other hand, in a drawing in the Louvre which is attributed to van der Weyden and which represents a direct continuation of the great drama, i.e. The Carrying of the Dead Christ. This composition reappears in the large triptych by the Frankfort Master in the church in Watervliet (between Gand and Bruges). Finally, a large relief carved in wood, which was recently acquired by the Detroit Institute of Arts, is related to the Louvre drawing.

The posture of the Magdalen is the balancing echo of John's in the veiled symmetry of the composition. Despite a substantial modelling of her body the design is essentially less sculptural than in the figures of the first group (e.g. Mary). The effort to bring all parts of the figure into one plane may be perceived in the exaggerated tilting of her torso. Consequently, her right arm is awkwardly raised more than is necessary to indicate its receding into space. The Magdalen is conceived as a high-relief form, whereas the figures of the first group may be regarded as sculptures in the round. The style of the hands is less intensely naturalistic than the hands of Mary; this is shown in a more abstract execution of the wrinkles and wooden-stick fingers. There is something mannered and intellectually detached, as it were; hardly the product of a close observation of a real gesture of clasped fingers.[6]

The area between the Magdalen and Nicodemus seems to me to be the weakest in the whole painting and it deviates in many ways from the compositional principles, so lucidly expressed throughout the scene. There are too many forms crowded into a narrow space and the overall high-relief manner is confused and difficult to comprehend.[7] This undesirable effect is mainly caused by the figure of the man holding a jar of ointment. It is quite probable that he does not belong to the original concept of the picture and was added only during its execution. The man's left hand is stretched forward as a means of asserting his importance in the composition. The thrusting gesture bypasses the intermediate plane of the Magdalen's hands in apparent disregard for the gradual organization of masses.[8] The brushwork is smooth and unemotional and the film is thin as in the figures of the second group.

The entire composition has the character of absolute clarity, finality and perfection. Everything is placed with an ultimate validity and nothing can be moved even by a fraction of an inch.[9] This quality, however, seems to be

6   It should be noted that in 1847 Jacob Burckhardt (*Handbuch der Geschichte der Malerei*) criticized the wringing hands of the Magdalen as being too mannered, although he otherwise thought that the grouping was boldly and successfully conceived. Similarly, Crowe and Cavalcassele in the *History of Early Flemish Painting* (1875) commented on the hand-wringing gesture: "... tendency to exaggerate the expression of suffering, to bring the treatment to a height at which it becomes unnatural. The figures have Rogier's usual defects, the hard outlines, the emaciation, and fall short of true feeling. Nevertheless, the head of Christ is not lacking in a certain grave beauty ..."

7   A "classical" demonstration of the sculptural principle distinguishing the composition as a whole may be seen in the successive, unobstructed arrangement of the following: the skull, Mary's hand, John's foot, her body, her left hand, Christ's hand, Joseph's right leg, his fur mantle, the cross and the ladder. These forms in their step-like recession, suggest well the idea of orderly depth.

8   A similar instance of projecting into the space forward exists in the tip of John's belt which points out of the plane of the picture. The *pentimento* shows that the belt was originally narrower.

9   Friedländer, *op. cit.*, II, p. 22: "Nichts darin ist verstellbar, verschiebbar, nichts

lacking in the area just mentioned around the hands of the Magdalen: the shapes are too casually delineated by overlapping and the resulting insignificant portions lack strength of design and are plastically meaningless. Neither the light nor the dark surfaces are resolved here in a "grand" and monumental manner as in the rest of the composition.

The rhythm of the composition is powerful and grave. Angularity prevails and the curvilinear rhythm is confined to the bent figures of John and the Magdalen which bracket the group. The parallel construction of the bodies of Mary and Christ brings them up to an equal level of thematic, psychological and expressive importance.[10]

The preoccupation with the phenomena of light is not consistent throughout the group. Modelling by means of light is most emphatic in the collapsed body of Mary. Her left hand even casts a shadow on the strongly lighted drapery on her hip. Similarly, a shadow on the foot of the youth which is cast by the ladder has been reproduced. A cavernous space darkens the very center of the panel between the legs of Joseph, and the ample drapery of Mary's mantle penetrates its shadow. On the other hand, the right-hand part of the painting is bathed in a more diffused light and the distinction between light and shade is less pronounced.[11] This corroborates the variegated situation as far as the brushwork, color and forms are concerned.

There is little doubt that the artist who conceived the highly sculptural figures and painted them with bold impasto strokes, yet with a loving precision, and aimed at the maximum expression of fullness of volume and of tangibility was the originator of the design of the group. There is an unanimity between the characteristics of the composition, the language of the powerful and sculptural figures and the bold technique and brushwork. The faces of the first group have an earthy quality and are not very handsome but are endowed with psychological intensity and character. A sensuous vitality permeates the vigorous forms. The painter took delight in the naturalistic rendering of the various materials and substances (such as the face of Nicodemus, the hands of Mary,

---

anders zu denken. ... Jede Figur scheint gerade dort sein zu müssen, wo sie ist."

10   This was noted by Walter Ueberwasser, *Rogier van der Weyden*, London 1947, p. 7.

11   Not all the figures cast their shadow on the gold background, but I do not find this evidence conclusive enough for any differentiation, as I consider the technique used to register them as additional. Somehow, I have the feeling that the technique of toning down the intensity of a gold background by covering it with small dabs of semi-opaque brown paint, which are used in a more condensed conformation for the cast shadows, is incompatible with Campin's solid textures and is more related to the abstract spirit of van der Weyden's creations. A supporting piece of evidence is to be found in the analogous treatment of a portion of the gold background in the polyptych at Beaune and in the Madonna and Child in the Hutington Collection in San Marino, California. (Panofsky, *op. cit.*, Fig. 370).

the garment of the youth, the ladder, the skull and the plants). He was interested in the impact of light. His colors are well saturated and their arrangement is calculated to give the fullest effect. The shading of the flesh parts is in cool tones, mostly silvery grayish.

The style of the second artist is never in direct contrast to that of the first, as they both use a common formal vocabulary. Moreover, many features such as the interest in the naturalistic rendering of fabrics is a trend shared by leading artists of the time. Nevertheless, his own distinct "écriture graphique" may be recognized—mainly in John and the Magdalen— although he probably painted some areas over a guiding underdrawing or perhaps even over the painting of the first artist. His types are more elegant and emaciated, the forms are less voluminous, more linear and decorative. His realism is less intense, and mannered forms may be perceived; for instance, Magdalen's clasped hands form an unnatural conformation; the mantle clinging to her hip only by a miracle is a decorative, abstract device. The paint film is unemotionally thin and structurally less complex and the colors are rather warm. The brushstrokes lack compactness and a conviction about the essence of the things to be represented, as if they had been made by somebody whose descriptive style is not quite appropriate to the creating of monumental forms (viz. the mantle of John). The painter was apparently not at ease in large-scale painting. Though details such as the tears are painted expertly, his handwriting gives an impression of limited experience, hesitancy and caution.

That very same spirit of Campin's genius and those idiomatic formal and technical pecularities which we have encountered in scrutinizing his works are present in the major part of the Descent painting. This statement may seem a fanciful and heretical assertion, but I hope that a careful study of my arguments will result in removing the seeming air of absurdity since the painting is generally regarded as by van der Weyden. One unique technical detail establishes the presence of Campin's hand in the Descent. We have observed in the examination of the Frankfort "Bad Thief" panel that the body hair was first painted with white paint and the impasto white lines were covered with a black semi-glaze stroke. This identical procedure to achieve the materiality of the hair was used in the Escorial panel on the legs of Christ. I believe that very special technical procedures of this kind, which often seem to be without visible importance (as this one), are a genuine innate manifestation of the artistic personality, as they often have meaning only to the originator. They are least likely to be taken over by a follower or a pupil. On the other hand, facial and hand types, though very important to connoisseurship, may be more easily appropriated by some other artist.

As I implied above, this painting appears to have been finished by another artist who was a close follower of the master's style but whose own artistic expressions may, nevertheless, be readily recognized. I believe that it was Roger van der Weyden who endowed the features of John, Joseph, the Magdalen, the man on the right and, possibly, the young woman with his own vision of human-ity, but he was not responsible for those other figures nor did he conceive the composition.[12] It is indeed one of the ironies of fate that the painting lived on and continues to live on as the chief work of an artist who, as I believe, merely completed a monumental idea conceived by his master. It was Campin's unjust fate that his name was erased from the memory of generations to come—just as a name inscribed by a stylus on a wax tablet can be removed without leaving a trace.

Yet human perception is, despite everything, a sensitive seismograph of subtle and keen sensations. The majority of writers on the subject were inevi-tably aware of the exceptional position and uniqueness of this painting in the reconstructed *oeuvre* of van der Weyden. They sensed the discrepancies and remarked again and again on the peculair qualities of the composition, the sculptural feeling, the unusually sensuous vitality and its startling similarity to the Flémalle's works in Frankfort.[13] However, the *aqua pura* of this clairvoyant

12   The highly reassuring feeling of a *communio viatorum* in the quest for unique-ness in artistic creation was engendered by the discovery that the differences between the two artistic personalities had been stated in a similar manner by the art critic Roger Fry. In his reaction to the theory of Emile Renders: "The Flémalle, van der Weyden Ques-tion", *The Burlington Magazine,* 61, 1932, p. 117 f., he lucidly summed up the art of these two painters as follows: "Flémalle with the specifically painter-like way of under-standing things, with an imaginative sense of the total visual quality, of the impact of light, of the bulk and volume of the object, of its material quality... Van der Weyden ... a man of an utterly different temperament, a man lacking the specific painter's sensuality, a man whose chief interest is in the nature of his imagery, and of its dramatic import, and relatively unimaginative about visual values. One of the greatest, the most dramatic illustrators of the day, but definitely not a painter.—Flémalle paints with a dense rich paste which has great luminosity, ... unctuous gem-like brilliancy; he gives us the full body of things.—Roger paints thinly, evenly and with far less expression of the light and shade, the relief and volume.—(Flémalle) ... material qualities are detailed with lingering delight.—(Roger) ... merely neatly executed.—Flémalle's land-scape ... is full of fascinated wonder of effects of light and shade.—Roger's landscape ... spreads in quite conventional lines across the background ... (is) not passionately seen. He is only excited where psychological and literary values are in focus ... elsewhere he is more or less conscientiously decorative. Flémalle is ... a more vividly imaginative, altogether odder, stranger type of mind".
There is an engraving by the Master of the Banderoles (Hamburg, Kunsthalle) where the motifs from the two great Descents from the Cross—the Escorial and the other, known in he Liverpool copy, were fused. The combination of the two apparently famous compositions may have been conceivably based upon an authentic drawing from Campin's studio and supports my conclusion that both are creations of Campin.
13   Friedländer, *op. cit.,* p. 24: "Die Kreuzabnahme ist wegen des ungewohnten Figurenmassstabes sowie wegen der beispiellosen Anlage, des einmaligen Kompositions-gedankens, mit anderen Schöpfungen Rogiers nicht ohne weiteres vergleichbar."— Paul Jamot, "Roger van der Weyden et le prétendu Maître de Flémalle," *Gazette des Beaux-*

feeling about the connection of the two was blurred in the reflections of the
historians of art because of their unquestioning trust in the testimony of a late

---

Arts, 1928, vol. II, p. 264 (about the Descent): "Même type des figures, même rapport
particulier de ces figures au champ de la composition, même dessin puissant et ressenti,
même sens du relief, même composition sculpturale, même fond d'or. Ce sont les ad-
mirables panneaux conservés à l'Institut Staedel de Francfort."—p. 267: "parmi les
tableaux aujourd'hui attribués au Maître de Flémalle, les plus beaux et les plus caractéristiques sont justement ceux qui se rapprochent le plus de ce chef-d'œuvre (la Descente)."
—p. 270: "... il s'y exprime pleinement et tout entier avec une force et pathétique que
nous ne trouverons ensuite au même degré dans aucune peinture de sa main."—p. 276:
"Et voilà une raison de plus, assez forte de croire que les tableaux antérieurs à la Descente
(i.e. Merode) où cette figure de la Vierge commence par s'annoncer, puis s'affirme de
plus en plus avec tous ses traits caractéristiques sont de celui qui a fait le chef-d'oeuvre
où elle atteint à sa plus parfaite beauté d'expression. (i.e. the Descent)"—Emille Renders,
"L'énigme du Maître de Flémalle," *La Revue d'art*, 1929, p. 199: "Par quel phénomène
surnaturel la toute première oeuvre attribuée au grand Roger est et restera éternellement
son chef-d'oeuvre?"—E. Renders, *La solution du problème van der Weyden, Flémalle,
Campin* (Bruges, 1931), vol. II, p. 72, Pl. 43. He recognizes the similarity of the Bad
Thief in Frankfort and Christ in the Escorial (B, C) and contrasts them with the figures
of Christ in the Vienna and Berlin Crucifixions (A, D): "En B et C les formes anatomi-
ques plus opulentes, en opposition avec la gracilité des deux figures précédentes (A, D).
Même concept anatomique dans les lignes générales ... apparaît clairement une écriture
graphique similaire ... aux ombres grises et si transparentes, personne n'oserait contester
que ces deux figures ne soient pas d'une même et unique palette."—Pl. 74 (the feet of
the Bad Thief (A) and of Christ in the Escorial (D)): "... forme des orteils est iden-
tique."—Pl. 50 (the heads of the Escorial and Frankfort Marys): "un même type."—p.
81: "Si nous ne savions par des textes que le panneau de l'Escurial est de Roger, la
critique, depuis bien longtemps, aurait classé d'office cette oeuvre colossale sur la liste
des oeuvres de Flémalle, et l'eut jointe à celles de Francfort qui sont d'un sentiment et
d'une facture égaux."—Theodor Musper, *Untersuchungen zu Rogier van der Weyden und
Jan van Eyck*, Stuttgart, 1948, p. 25: "Sie (the Prado and Liverpool Descents) zeigen die
Entwicklung auf so einleuchtend und so logisch, dass es unmöglich ist, in ihnen länger
die Werke zweier Maler zu sehen."—W. Ueberwasser, *op. cit.*, p. 14: ... innovations in-
troduced by the "Master of Flémalle" ... for instance, the realistically painted head of
Nicodemus (in the Descent)."—H. Beenken, *op. cit.*, p. 27 (about the colors in the
Escorial): "... im engsten Anschluss dagegen an die der grossen Einzelfigurenbilder
Campins in Frankfurt."—p. 49: "Die stilistischen Beziehungen zumal zu den grossen in
Frankfurt hängenden Tafeln des älteren so überaus enge sind dass man gerade die hier
behauptete Identität des "Meisters von Flémalle" und Rogiers am deutlichsten erweisen
zu können geglaubt hat. In der Tat ist in zahllosen Einzelheiten die lineare Struktur, die
künstlerische Handschrift so nahe verwandt dass diese Identität durchaus glaubhaft er-
scheinen könnte."—Leo van Puyvelde, *La peinture flamande au siècle des van Eyck*
(Paris, 1953), p. 143: "Pourtant elle (La Descente) ne nous semble pas constituer le
chief-d'oeuvre du peintre ... il (Roger) n'abandonna pas encore la préoccupation de ce
dernier (Flèmalle) pour la vision sculpturale et la multiplicité des tons. ... Il est bien loin
cependant d'atteindre dans ce domaine la complète expression de sa personalité."—E.
Panofsky, *op. cit.*, p. 169: "Veronica is as relatively Rogerian as Roger's Descent is relatively Flémallesque."—p. 258: "Descent is ... animated by a rich unrepressed and, in
spite of the subject, almost sensuous vitality soon to give way to austere unwordliness."

document. The instinctive recognition was thought to be a misleading *Fata Morgana,* so that complex and ingenious speculations seeking to explain and rationalize the discrepancies of style and to fit them into a preconceived pattern of evolution were expounded instead.

In my illustration the specific distribution of the various parts of the Descent between the two artists is given, based on an examination of the paint layer, personal handwriting, style and quality of workmanship.[14] The lower part of the figure of John, i.e. the feet, the hand and the lower part of the drapery up to the knees, is by Campin. Van der Weyden completed the figure, probably following the tracing of the master.[15] John's physiognomy is his own invention. The weeping older woman and Mary were entirely painted by Campin. The young woman was started by Campin, who finished her dress, perhaps with the exception of her right sleeve, but van der Weyden, who painted her face, seems here to have followed closely the underdrawing of Campin, as is seen in the voluminous concept of the head. Christ's body is by Campin but was touched up, mainly on the arms, by van der Weyden who also painted the shroud; his legs, the crown of thorns and most of the face remain unobliterated by the latter's intervention. The figure of Joseph of Arimathea is by Campin but the coat and the face are by van der Weyden, perhaps painted thinly over an existing face by Campin. The young man, the fluttering cloth, the cross and the ladder were painted by Campin. The figure of Nicodemus is by Campin except for the foot on the left.[16] The Magdalen was painted by van der Weyden, most probably in accordance with the main outline of Campin's underdrawing, which Roger, however, subjected to certain variations. The hands are typically Rogerian: the long fingers are clasped in a stiff, cramped pose, with no flexing of the third joints—very much like, for example, the hands of John the Baptist in the Bracque triptych in the Louvre.[17] The man with the jar of ointment was painted by Roger, and, I believe, to his own design as an addition to the original composition. Finally, the ground, including the plants on the left,

14   Unfortunately, there are no X-ray and infra-red photographs to corroborate the distinctions made here.

15   The motif cherished by van der Weyden, namely the posture of crossed legs which he preferred in his figures of John, exists in the Descent in the figure of Nicodemus but, strangely enough, not in John's. The "open" position of John's legs is most probably Campin's design.

16   It is very difficult to recognize the authorship of the heavy brocaded mantle, since any execution of highly ornate pattern, here rendered in impasto hatching, tends to become mechanical and, thus, any mark of personality elusive.

17   Beenken, *op. cit.* Fig. 78. Fr. Winkler noted that Roger often stylized the hands in an almost affected manner (*The Art Quarterly,* 1950, p. 216). The thumbs are pointed and the nails lack accent, as they are not encircled by modelling shadows. This is the type of finger discussed in connection with Veronica's hands in Frankfort. Campin's type of finger, described in the same place, is used in the Descent on Mary's and John's hands.

the skull and the femur bone, is by Campin. As insignificant part of the ground on the right may be by van der Weyden, as a lesser intensity in the rendering suggests.

The humanity created by Robert Campin, which we find in his paintings, has congregated here in this tragic scene. Mary's face is a more masterly and advanced portrayal of Mary in the Merode and London paintings—a Mary who had aged in the meantime. The young man is akin to the earthy types of the two men standing under the cross in the Frankfort panel. Nicodemus is strongly reminiscent of the two portraits, in the Berlin Museum and in the Thyssen Collection in Lugano, which will be examined as possibly meaningful. The Christ is very far removed from the thin, emaciated fragile Christ consistently favored by van der Weyden.[18] The figure is closer to the massive body of the Thief and to Christ in the Trinity in grisaille, both in Frankfort, although not all the elements of the features are akin, e.g. the beard.

On the other hand, John is in the true tradition of Roger's slender and solicitous Johns. The Magdalen is repeated in a drawing in the Louvre after a Rogerian composition of the Carrying of the Dead Christ and in the Descent from the Cross in Niederwaroldern.[19] The figure of Joseph of Arimathea was re-used later by Roger in his Italianate Entombment in the Uffizi. The balding man with the jar is likewise a Rogerian character. These types continued to appear in the creative paintings of the Rogerian school long after the death of Campin (1444), whereas the robust race of the first group died out with his own departure. The fact that only some of the types survived is still another indication that Campin was the spiritual father and painter of the first group of figures in the Deposition.

I may be accused perhaps of a mania for dissection, of a psychosis for seeing differences and alien intervention in practically all the paintings discussed. In reply to any criticism I would venture to suggest that collaboration by various hands in works of art of this period was actually far greater than we realize.[20]

It may seem odd that there should be participation by a second hand often in small, unrelated areas. Is it not more logical to expect such participation in rather larger units such as ground, landscape, etc.? In the case of the Prado Deposition no rational pattern governing the collaboration seems to exist. It is

18   E.g. in the Crucifixion triptych in Vienna, Kunsthistorisches Museum.

19   Musper, *op. cit.*, Figs. 53 and 30.

20   Art history ventures very little in this respect beyond the recorded instances of collaboration of two artists such as S. Martini and L. Memmi in the Uffizi Annunciation, and Verrocchio and Leonardo da Vinci in the Baptism of Christ. Analysis of the paint structure has been applied only to a few works so far and a rigorous differentiation from this point of view would, it is to be hoped, clearly define the artistic profiles of many important masters. A study of the works attributed to van der Weyden himself would possibly yield interesting revelations; I can quote, as an instance, the diverse appearance of the head and hand of the Man with an Arrow in Brussels on the X-ray photograph.

my opinion that Campin had completed some shapes, whereas other shapes or areas were left untouched.[21] His precise underdrawing perfectly enabled him, if he wanted to, to work on units isolated one from the other. He did not necessarily have to complete large continuous areas—an approach which perhaps suited his own inclinations and, from the practical point of view, allowed him to work with one color at a time.[22] This procedure was by no means isolated and unique. An excellent illustration of this approach is afforded by two unfinished paintings by Michelangelo in the National Gallery in London—Madonna with Angels and Youth John the Baptist, and the Entombment (Nos. 790 and 809). The completely finished parts border on untouched parts revealing the gesso and preparatory drawing. The solitary character of Michelangelo's creation, and perhaps a reverence by his contemporaries for the unique and individual in a work of art, prevented the *lacunae* from being completed afterwards, so that we have the paintings as Michelangelo had left them.[23] On the other hand, the collective character of workshop production—and such a situation probably existed in Campin's studio—combined with the need to deliver the commissions in time and in a completed state would not have allowed

21   It appears that painting imbued with naturalistic connotations, such as was Campin's art, had moved further and further away from the traditional techniques of the preceding period, as represented by the broad and general type of underpainting with conventional colors such as the greenish tint of the Italo-Byzantine tradition for underpainting the flesh, ochre for the furniture and conventionally restricted colors for the garments. In this older, conceptual method, the modelling in the top paint layers gave the shapes their final formulation and the elaboration of the features was effected at this stage only.

22   Coarse, sketchy underdrawing with thick, erratic brushstrokes was alien to Campin, but it was used by his collaborator in the left-hand wing of the Merode triptych, by the painter of the London Magdalen and by the copyist of his own Trinity composition in the Louvain Trinity. (Johannes Taubert, "La Trinité du Musée de Louvain. Une nouvelle methode de critique des copies", *Bulletin de l'Institut Royal du Patrimoine Artistique*, vol. II, 1959, p. 22, Fig. 1; p. 31, Fig. 5). This type, much less unique, was used subsequently by a number of fifteenth-century painters (e.g. in a Roger-inspired Nativity altarpiece at the Cloisters in New York).

23   Philip Hendy, *Art Treasures of the National Gallery, London,* New York 1955, p. 90. The body of the Child is provided with all the modelling and yet the adjacent drapery of Mary is only drawn with black hatching. The apex of her coiffure is left altogether unpainted, although the rest of the hair is finished. In the Entombment, the hands of the figure on the left are entirely unpainted, although her lilac dress and face are completely painted. Similarly the body of Christ was completed, but the area for the fingers of Nicodemus supporting him at the armpit was, oddly enough, left empty. The sash of the young man is also unpainted. The hand of Christ itself has been completely painted, whereas the hand next to it has been left unpainted.—Manuscript illuminations occasionally reveal this sectional working procedure. Examples of this are to be seen in several partially finished miniatures in a Bohemian Bible from 1402 in the Plantin-Moretus Museum in Antwerp. Codex No. 15.1. (Z. Drobná, *Gothic Drawing* (Prague), Figs. 108-11; Fols. 171v-174v.)

gaps to be left unfinished. We do not know the circumstances of the execution of works commissioned from Campin. Perhaps the work in progress had to be interrupted in favor of a more rewarding commission or as a result of the master's absence due to travel, sickness, etc., at a time crucial to the completion of the ordered panel. Or a commission may have been cancelled.

The portions in Campin's paintings completed by a different hand are not limited to subordinate details or areas of secondary importance or to specific parts, which would point to a division of work by specialization.[24] It is definitely a question of the completion of unfinished work in most cases and only exceptionally it is a question of an overpainting (as the scheme of the donors, for example, may have required it). Hence some form of equality must have existed between the collaborators and the master.

Let us review briefly documentary evidence of Roger van der Weyden's authorship of the Descent from the Cross from the Escorial. His name is mentioned for the first time in conjunction with the painting in 1574 in the inventory of the Spanish King Philip II after it reached Spain.[25] Certainly, nobody can maintain that a document dated some hundred and forty years after the creation of the painting has an uncontestable validity. We do not know how well founded the attribution made to Roger in 1574 was. It may have been based on a written record in the town of Louvain but it may equally have been the continuance of a mere tradition which may have lost its accuracy in the course of four generations. The question I am asking here is, how much credence can be given to non-contemporaneous documents.

I do not intend to deny the validity of the attribution, at least not entirely, but I do wish to amend it partly. I certainly concede that if written documents from the fifteenth century were to be found, the name of Roger would most probably be mentioned, for I am convinced that he worked on the painting.

24   There is nothing in these paintings of that systematic and specialized collaboration of a J. Patinir and Quentin Matsys and G. David or Rubens and J. Fyt.

25   Carl Justi, "Altflandrische Bilder in Spanien und Portugal", *Zeitschrift für bildende Kunst*, 1886, p. 97. The Regent of the Netherlands, Mary of Hungary, paid a high price for he painting in 1556. (Viz. Otto von Simson, "Compassio and Coredemptio in Roger van der Weyden's Descent from the Cross", *The Art Bulletin*, 1953, p. 9.) She commissioned the painter Michel Coxcie in 1569 to paint an exact copy with the intention of donating it to the church of the Notre-Dame-hors-les-murs in Louvain where the original had stood. However, this painting was also shipped to Spain (we know that the original entered El Escorial in 1574), as it was mentioned by Argote de Molina in 1582 as being in the Capilla del Rey in the old Prado. Recently, since the Civil War, the two have changed places and the original is now in the Prado Museum (No. 2825), while the Coxcie copy is in the Escorial (No. 1893). There is yet another copy (No. 1814) in the Prado which came from the monastery of St. Maria de los Angeles in Madrid. According to the records, King Philip sent the painter, Anton Pupiler, to Louvain in 1567, for nine months to copy the altarpiece and this purports to the latter copy.

But I do not agree that he was the author. He only finished a painting more than half completed by his teacher, Robert Campin. Unfortunately, the contract for his important work, which would give us the name of the artist who was commissioned to paint it, is not in our possession. If there had been some uncertainty about the author at the time when Mary of Hungary negotiated the purchase, it may be expected that the name of Roger, very well known and celebrated as one of the greatest painters of the fifteenth century,[26] would have been asserted, especially in view of the high price involved. The painting had been famous since the time of its completion, and the scene had been reproduced in many copies, both faithful and free.[27]

Quite naturally, we may ask why would so important a painting be started by one artist and finished by another, and be known as the work of the second. Here nothing can be established which would go beyond mere hypothesis. However, certain circumstances may be considered which would indicate an explanation in the direction which I now propose to explore.

Most writers place the Deposition in the fourteen-thirties as an early work of Roger.[28] We know that it must have been finished before the year 1443 when it was copied in the Edelheer altarpiece in St. Peter's in Louvain. It is quite plausible to assume that it must have been started several years earlier, because a triptych of this importance and size could hardly be designed and executed in, say, less than one year. We may perhaps push the date considerably further back and connect it with the record of the substantial investment made in Tournai securities by Roger on October 20, 1435. The money may have come from the money received for the large triptych, which was certainly a considerable sum.[29] (My thesis does not contradict the general assumption that it was delivered as Roger's work, as I shall argue shortly.)

26   Cardinal Nicholas Cusanus called him "maximus pictor". Facius in his *De viris illustribus* from 1455-57 included him among the four most celebrated painters.

27   The first copy, the Edelheer altarpiece from 1443 in St. Peter's in Louvain, simplified the shape of the panel by eliminating its elevated center. There is a copy in Berlin from 1488. The Master of the St. Bartholomew Altarpiece from Cologne also followed the composition in his Descent in the Louvre. Another copy, this time with a landscape background, is in the Johnson Collection in Philadelphia. A print from 1563 by C. Cort, provided with Roger's name, is evidence of its wide popularity. The two copies in Spain date from 1567 and 1569. Old attributions must often be taken *cum grano salis*; Molanus, for example, maintained that Roger painted the Edelheer retable, which is, of course, impossible. (Friedländer, *op. cit.*, p. 17). One must remain cautious of "wholesale" attributions of famous names.

28   If one chooses to believe that the Granada altarpiece must antedate 1438, then one is confronted with the baffling realisation that a profound change must have taken place in Roger's imagination, style, and whole temperament after he conceived the Descent. This places a great strain on one's credulity and is, to say the least, highly improbable. The appraisal of Roger's evolution needs a new, fresh look.

29   Panofsky, *op. cit.*, p. 257.

It is not unreasonable to recognize in Nicodemus a portrait of a real person-
age. Its similarity to a man's portrait in Lugano is striking, only the fat double
chin being diminished in size. This may be an idealization or it may represent
features of the same man somewhat earlier. It has been suggested that the
Lugano portrait represents Robert the Masmines, Counsellor and General of the
Burgundian Dukes, John the Fearless and Philip the Good. Of the two possibilities, namely that the author of the Deposition simply re-used uninten-
tionally one of his portrait drawings for the type of the thick-set Nicodemus or
that he intentionally represented the high official in a prominent place, I am
inclined to favor the second.[30] The superb gold brocade mantle with fancy
sleeves is more appropriate for a prominent court figure than for a bourgeois
member of the Archers' confraternity in Louvain.[31] *Pentimenti* indicate changes
in the shape of Nicodemus' black headgear, and the deciphering of its original
shape will be perhaps illuminating as to the man's status in society. If it really
is a portrait of Robert de Masmines under the guise of Nicodemus, it follows,
firstly, that we ought perhaps to date the Descent (or, at least, the beginning
of the work) from before the death of Robert de Masmines in 1430. (Unless
we consider the altarpiece a posthumous *ex voto*.) Secondly, we should perhaps
ask ourselves whether the huge altarpiece was commissioned by the confraternity of Archers at all. (It would not be difficult to add two small painted crossbows and thus provide it *ex post* with a link with the Archers' confraternity.
These two little emblems are also painted on the Berlin copy from 1488, but
not on the Edelheer panel.)

Now let lus look at some events from the life of Robert Campin. He became
a sympathizer with the revolutionary progressive faction which took over the
rule of the city government in Tournai in 1423, became Dean of the painters'
guild and was a member of one of the three City Councils from 1425 until
1428.[32] This party represented the interests of the underprivileged class of
craftsmen and young intellectuals against the perennial rule of the patricians,
prosperous merchants and clergy.

At the same time, in a complex play of political balances, this party was loyal

30 Nicodemus in the Rogerian drawing of the Carrying of the Dead Christ in the
Louvre seems to assume the features of Chancellor Rolin in his mature years. (Reproduced in Panofsky, Fig. 392). The chief figures in the compositions, like Nicodemus
here, were perhaps occasionally portraits of persons in some way connected with the
commissioning of the paintings.

31 From the tiny crossbows hanging on either side of the Gothic tracery in the
corners it was ascertained that the panel was made for the Arbalisters' company in
Louvain. W. Ueberwasser, *op. cit.*, p. 8, thought that "a gentleman of the town of Louvain (one that everyone knew) took part in the Descent."

32 Panofsky, *op. cit.*, p. 154. However, Maurice Houtart merely states that Campin
was a vice dean of the guild of goldsmiths (*Jacques Daret, peintre tournaisien du XVe
siècle*, Tournai, 1908, p. 11).

to the French crown against the Burgundian State.[33] It certainly sheds light on the social conscience of Campin that he should have sided with the democratic party, since he would rather have been expected to favor the other side in view of his business interests as a painter.

After the defeat of the radical party, Campin apparently was ostracized in 1429 from any public office.[34] It was on his pupil, Jacques Daret, that the office of the Dean of the painters' guild was conferred the moment his apprenticeship was over. Surprisingly to us, he was elected the very day, October 18, 1432, on which he was elevated to the rank of the masters, though he was still young and inexperienced.[35]

In these circumstances, we may easily understand—if we elaborate our thoughts further—why the Archers' confraternity, composed of wealthy patricians of Louvain, would look for some pretext to cancel their commission to a "subversive" painter who had taken active part in a movement directed against their fellow patricians at Tournai who had fled in great numbers from the town during the five years reign of the popular party. If we favor, on the other hand, the identification of Nicodemus with Robert de Masmines, then a similar dislike on the part of this court official may be presupposed. The work may have been left in an unfinished state after his death in 1430. Finally, the scandal involving the married Campin with a certain Leurance Polette in 1432 may also have had some bearings on the fate of the commission of the triptych.[36]

33   I should like to make a comment with regard to a detail used again and again in the arguments of the Campin-Van der Weyden controversy. People speculated why "Master Rogier" was presented at his visit to Tournai in 1426 with a larger offering of wine than Jan van Eyck himself received a little later on the same occasion. The reason why the famous artist got less may perhaps have been a reflection of the anti-Burgundian feelings of the town council at that time. After all, van Eyck was a court painter and diplomat of the Duke of Burgundy.

34   Two fines were imposed on him on March 21, 1429; he also had to make a pilgrimage to Saint Gilles in Southern France and was deprived for ever "d'être en loi et en office", which practically ruined his career. Houtart, op. cit., p. 13.

35   Yet Campin's advice was still sought, even afterwards: we know that he helped to draw up the terms of a contract for an altarpiece in St. Nicholas' in 1434. In 1438 he made cartoons for a large canvas hanging portraying scenes from the life of St. Peter, but one of his former pupils was commisioned to paint it.

36   The verdict condemning him to banishment from the town for one year was commuted upon the personal intervention of the reigning princess, Jacqueline of Holland, Bavaria and the Hainaut. (Houtart, op. cit., p. 8). This may be evidence of the recognition of Campin's talent among the nobility, but the gallant act of coming to the aid of an acknowledged anti-Burgundian may also have had a political significance, since she was in constant difficulties with Philip the Good. Houtart thought that an intervention of such a nature often indicated that the beneficiary was in the process of executing a work for the intervening person. Panofsky (op. cit., p. 155) telescopes the two separate prosecutions of Campin in 1429 and 1432 into one event.

Let us pursue tentatively as a working theory the identification of Nicodemus with Robert de Masmines. If the contract was broken on some pretext, Campin would probably have stopped the work on the altarpiece in 1429 or 1430. The well advanced painting would have been completed by his pupil Roger van der Weyden when he was given a commission to paint an altarpiece for the Archers' group in Louvain, after he had received in 1432 the tittle of Master with the right to conclude commissions for himself. He would possibly have delivered the panel before 1435. He might even have acted as a cover agent for Campin, who, according to the sentence was barred from concluding commissions and might have become unacceptable to many patrons. The whole affair may simply have been a face-saving transaction, and Roger, besides completing the unfinished areas, thus may have lightly covered over other, more or less finished areas (i.e. Christ's chest and arms and Joseph's face?).

These incidents in Campin's life, together with other unknown circumstances, may have a bearing on the obscurity of Campin as a great artist even in almost contemporary writings. I have a feeling that Campin's association with the revolt in Tournai in the third decade of the century had a fatal bearing on his fame and wide recognition.[37] It may be that public opinion in the Low Countries, articulated by the patricians and the clergy, conspired to silence his fame and popularity, since patricians and clergy were indignant about his deviations from the moral code and annoyed at his taking sides with the classes which were revolting against the old, established political and social orders. Likewise, the officials of the ducal court may have adopted a hardened and vengeful attitude to the artist who supported the enemies of the "Etats du Grand-Duc d'Occident". Foreign writers on art matters, especially Italians, had to rely on information reaching them from upper-class travellers, merchants and diplomats, who might have been prejudiced.[38]

When Albrecht Dürer visited Bruges in 1520, he wrote admiring notes about the paintings of a great unknown Fleming, in addition to those of "Rudiger".[39] Why would a great painter become unknown in an art-loving society after only two or three generations? The oral tradition could be expected still to know

37   Ch. de Tolnay felt similarly about this (*op. cit.*, p. 27). Almost a century later, the involvement of Tilman Riemenschneider in politics brought his career, it seems, to a catastrophic end. He was put in prison for his participation in the revolt against the Bishop of Würzburg in 1525 and there is no further record of his having received another commission. Max H. von Freeden, *Tilman Riemenschneider* (1954), p. 15.

38   An artistic appraisal is never free from personal overtones and was bound to have been less objective in times when access to information from distant areas was difficult. The cultural picture of a period could conceivably become one-sided in the light of contemporary testimonies, and the relative importance of various phenomena could be distorted.

39   Beenken, *op. cit.*, p. 13.

the name of the author of those large paintings, even if the written records were inaccessible to Dürer. It is rather as if a censor's veil had been drawn over the name of the painter. It is not wholly illogical to conceive that that great painter was Robert Campin himself. Perhaps that work admired by Dürer in the Ducal Chapel was his monumental altarpiece of the Descent from the Cross only a part of which survived in the Frankfort Bad Thief. It is perhaps not entirely a coincidence that the emblem of the town of Bruges is painted on the right-hand wing of the copy in Liverpool.[40]

The Deposition panel may be reconstructed as having been originally provided with closing wings. There is a note in the Escorial Inventory from 1574 of a pair of wings showing Four Evangelists with a Resurrection scene on their inner sides and paintings in black and white by a Spanish painter, Fernandez Mudo, on the exterior. Beenken (op.cit.) commented on the thematic and compositional strangeness of the lost wings.[41] As I stated above, the Escorial record by reason of its lateness, cannot be regarded as a document in the scientific sense as far as the origin of the panel is concerned. It is my opinion that this pair of wings is not necessarily the original pair. I believe that the original disposition of the wings more likely consisted of two pairs of large wings and one pair of small ones attached to the elevated center of the panel rather than of two huge wings of a shape similar to Broederlam's wings in Dijon. I therefore think that the altarpiece may have looked very similar in shape to the altarpiece of the Last Judgment in Beaune.

It is impossible to know whether the altarpiece stood complete with its wings in the chapel of Notre-Dame-hors-les-murs in Louvain when Mary of Hungary, daughter of Charles V, negotiated its acquisition for the King of Spain. They might already have been separated: a slight indication in this direction is the fact that there exist copies of the center panel only. What happened then to the wings? I venture the opinion that they stayed in the Low Countries. I came to

40 Friedländer, op. cit., p. 67. Further evidence may be furnished by the fact that the painter of a large Crucifixion in St. Sauveur's in Bruges, which dated from 1500, took over several figures from Campin's masterpiece. Ibid., p. 110. Campin's almost completely lost Descent known in the Liverpool copy must date, according to Hulin de Loo, from before 1430, because the illuminator of the Arenberg Hours (allegedly before 1430) used a modified version of the composition in one of his miniatures (Burlington Magazine, XIX). On the other hand, Panofsky pointed out that the Arenberg Hours, which can be dated at ca. 1435, reiterate a lost Campin Crucifixion, as does G. David's Crucifixion in Lugano. They are therefore not relevant to Campin's Descent, unless the Liverpool copy be a product of the telescoping of both the Crucifixion and the Descent which cannot be excluded.

41 Apart from the iconographic incongruity, it would be odd for a sixteenth-century Spanish painter to have painted the exterior of a famous Flemish altarpiece which could be presumed to have been completed, unless of course the Spaniard only overpainted some existing scenes which had been damaged.

the surprising conclusion that not all of the wings may have been lost. I like to explore the possibility that the panels with Veronica (and the Trinity on the reverse) and the Madonna in Frankfort may have made up one pair of the wings. Now that I have supplied my evidence to establish that Campin is the real author of the composition of the Descent, it is no longer surprising that "true" Campin paintings should form its wings. The sizes of the three panels, or more precisely their painted surfaces, tally with that of the Descent panel. The latter is 151 cm high at the sides, and the painted surfaces of the three panels vary only slightly in height between 148 cm and 148.9 cm.[42]

According to my hypothesis, the Madonna and Veronica panels probably formed the exterior pair of the wings, whereas the other pair of wings representing unknown subjects did not survive. If donors had been represented on the outer sides, then these panels could have been easily discarded when the altarpiece was dismembered, as I have ventured to hypothesize. The Frankfort panels would have been re-used for some other retable or shrine, as has been

___

42 The overall sizes of the three panels differ, however, and this would seem to preclude their association with the Descent panel. The discrepancy can, nevertheless, be readily explained. The largest of the three, namely the Madonna panel (68,2 x 159 cm) has an unpainted margin about 5 cm wide. Second in size is the Veronica (60,5 to 60,9 x 151,5 to 151,7 cm) and the unpainted margin here is only ca. 1,5 cm wide. It is very probable that, when the latter panel was cradled, the margins were trimmed down to a narrower strip to fit the rabbets of modern frames. Finally, the Trinity panel has no margins at all (its full size is 60,9 to 61,3 cm x 148,7 cm) and it seems that the edges of the painted surface were slightly trimmed down when the unpainted margin had been sawed off for some reason, since the damage along the edge has been retouched. Or was there a transfer of the painting from one wooden support to another? The present width of the Trinity is by some 2,5 or 3 cm respectively larger than that of the other two paintings and its height might originally also have been larger by a similar amount.

Does this automatically refute the theory that the Trinity once formed the reverse of the Veronica? The difference can, in fact, be accounted for, because paintings on the outer faces of the wings were occasionally slightly larger than those on the inner sides. This might have been motivated by a current taste for narrower framing of the closed ensemble. The frames of the Frankfort Madonna and Veronica must have been of considerable width since the unpainted margins, to be set into the frame, are themselves already up to 5 cm wide.

An identical width of frame was not always observed throughout all members of fifteenth-century altarpieces. The frame of the central panel was sometimes wider than that of the wings, e.g. the Last Supper by Dirk Bouts in St. Peter's in Louvain. (R. Lefève and F. van Molle, "La disposition originale des volets de la Dernière Cène de Bouts," *Bulletin de l'Institut Royal du Patrimoine Artistique*, vol. III, 1960, pp. 1-19.) Hence the frame of the Descent might have been still larger than that of the wings.

The panel with the Madonna is 14 mm thick, the Veronica panel is only 4 mm-5 mm and the Trinity panel is 12 mm. This would favor the theory that the latter two were arrived at by sawing through one two-sided panel. The missing two panels forming the intermediary pair of wings may be calculated, by allowing for the frames, to have been of a somewhat narrower size.

revealed by a much later repainting of the mourning Mary on the back of the Virgin's panel, but following in the general lines the original.[43]

The shallow space of a shrine represented in the Descent from the Cross was appropriately modified on the Frankfort wings to an analogously shallow strip of ground terminated by a wall covered with a hanging to keep the mood of spatial representation in harmony. The grass on the left in the Descent is as stereoscopic and tactile as is the lush floral carpet on the panels in Frankfort. It is also significant that a Trinity and a Mater Dolorosa in grisaille were painted on the exteriors of the wings of the Edelheer triptych in Louvain, which is, in its center section, a manifest copy of the Escorial Descent.[44] On the analogy of the juxtaposition of the Trinity and the Mater Dolorosa in the closed Edelheer triptych, we may infer that the Veronica panel was the wing on the extreme left because the Trinity, now separated, adorned most likely its reverse. The thematic coincidence of the two pairs of grisaille paintings strengthens my proposed reconstruction of the great triptych of the Descent from the Cross.

The head and hands of Veronica are in style, mood and technique identical to the figures of the second group in the Descent (John, Joseph, Magdalen, etc.). Consequently, it may be suggested that van der Weyden painted these portions of the Veronica panel. The same type of collaboration by the masters, Robert and Roger, exists in the Escorial and Frankfort panels, and this supplies additional evidence for their originally belonging together.

43   It must be conceded that a Nursing Virgin is iconographically as odd for a wing to a Descent from the Cross as the Veronica is highly appropriate.

44   Otto von Simson, *op. cit.*, p. 9ff, Fig. 4. The head of God the Father is very close to that in Frankfort but the gesture of Christ is almost the same as that in the Leningrad Trinity. The draftmanship is crude and it is probably the work of an assistant in Campin's studio who was familiar with various iconographic types created there. He added, probably of his own accord, the two angels standing on either side of the Trinity. He probably also added one more figure on the other grisaille painting; in the pendant he painted the grieving Mary in the arms of John. The wider proportions of the panels probably led him to increase the number of figures.

CHAPTER XIV

The Bracque Triptych in Paris

The Drawing of the Magdalen in London
The Drawing of the Thief in Cambridge, Mass.

The Bracque triptych in the Louvre can be placed with a reasonable precision as to date within Roger's *oeuvre*. The coat-of-arms of Jehan de Bracque of Tournai and his wife Catherine de Brabant date the triptych a few years before 1452, as the donor died that year. Looking at the retable, one is at once struck by the same acute feeling of discrepancy in the chromatic tuning of the constituent panels as was sensed in front of the Merode triptych. Here the situation is reversed: the center panel and the left-hand wing with John the Baptist are united in a warm color harmony, whereas the right-hand wing with the Magdalen is painted in a cool harmony of strong, brilliant luminous colors and silvery intermediates.[1] The difference is particularly striking in the painting of the complexion. The Magdalen's has all the characteristics of the skin color described in the above analysis of Campin's paintings—the flesh, of an almost translucent color, is daintily tinted with rose and modelled with cool grayish shadows. These shadows, however, are subordinated with absolute mastery to the idea of clearly expressing the stereoscopic volumes and never become too strong and independent. One can sense the delight the painter experienced in handling the color paste, which he smoothed to an enamel-like surface in the delicate textures of the skin and hair or else dabbed on the heavier textures of the dress

---

1 The colors produce a rich and *recherché* harmony. Magdalen's hair is slightly reddish, complexion is light creamy rose, her lips are fresh rosy pink. Her mantle is royal blue, the dress is gray, the ribbon of the belt is green. The sky is light and highly luminous.

and the bushy trees. The complexions of the figures on the other two panels are not as freshly pink, and the modelling is in brownish warm shades, in accordance with the procedure of Roger.

The degree of realistic intensity and accuracy is greater in the figure of the Magdalen than in the other four figures, which are more impersonal and typified.[2] The jar of ointment can be contrasted with that in the London Reading Magdalen. The voluminosity of the latter is exaggerated into an empty, uninteresting shape. The Louvre representation has a far more refined shape while retaining its sculptural feeling. The brocade of the Magdalen's sleeve is a little masterpiece of tactile values and the pin most realistically secures it to the garment.[3] A transparent veil gracefully encircles the face and the hat. A comparable use of this motif on the Frankfort Veronica is far less successful and adds to the confusion of the design of the head.

The hand of the Magdalen, though damaged, is articulate and sensitive, and is far superior to the hands of Christ and John the Evangelist, which are vulgar and badly drawn. The hands of the Virgin follow an established Rogerian scheme and thus appear more skilfully drawn. The right arm of John the Baptist is quite realistic, but his left hand has the stiff, mannered fingers characteristic of Roger's hands. His head seems to be superior to the three heads on the center panel. It coincides in type with the Baptist in the Medici Madonna in Frankfort but is turned to the three-quarters view; his right hand is identical in both instances. The harmony of the plum-violet color on the Baptist's mantle and the warm green on his garment seems to be a combination in vogue only in the second half of the fifteenth century.[4]

The distant landscape runs through the left-hand and center panels but is not connected at all with the landscape in the background of the Magdalen panel. The differences in the technique of the two parts of the landscape will be pointed out in the discussion of the X-ray evidence.

2 Panofsky (*op. cit.*, p. 276) remarks à propos of Magdalen: "And here is a restrained but almost voluptuous tenderness in the way in which her breasts are molded and her throat is made to shine through the transparent fabric of her veil." T. Musper speaks about "eine plastische Klarheit ... wie sie bis dahin selbst bei Rogier nicht vorkam."(*Op. cit.*, p. 54.)

3 We may perceive a less intense preoccupation with reality in this motif on the sleeve of the Magdalen in the Escorial Descent. The tight dress on both is laced in an identical way, through alternate holes, but the similarity does not go beyond the outer appearance.

4 This violetish tone is quite unlike the lilac of the International Style and seems to belong to a mannered phase of the painters' palette. This color may be seen, for instance, in Dirk Bout's altarpiece in Louvain from 1464-7 and in Hugo van der Goes' Adoration altarpiece in the Uffizi from 1476-8. Memlinc seems to have had a preference for it: viz. his Mystic Marriage in Bruges, Hospital of St. John, and two of his works in the National Gallery in London—a newly acquired retable and a wing panel with John the Baptist.

The inconsistency apparent at the first glance in the placing of the inscriptions throughout the triptych is corroborated by further examination. It is illogical that one and the same artistic temperament would use an elegant lay-out of fluttering inscriptions in two of the panels and a severe "Dorian" design of a straight line of inscription above the Magdalen's head in the third. The letters of the latter are more slender, their spacing is tighter and their types are not wholly identical to those in the other four inscriptions.[5] No one would dispute that the Magdalen's inscription is by another hand. Finally, the character of the texts themselves is different. On the Magdalen panel there is a quotation from the Gospel of St. John (12 : 3) of a factual content, whereas the other four inscriptions are biblical utterances of an exaltedly theological nature. This suggests inspiration in two differents spheres of thought.

There is a detail of seemingly little importance which, I feel, should not be overlooked. The artist provided the white hat of the Magdalen with an "invisible" inscription. It is barely visible since the Hebrew inscription is painted with white paint on the white hat. Its partial visibility is due only to the fact that the letters are executed with tiny pearls of thick white paint like filigree work. This peculiar representation is of double significance. First, it is a riddle, an indication of delight in a secret.[6] Second, it is a testimony to the

---

5   Cf. the letters G,A. The difference is certainly greater here than in the scrolls of the Dijon Nativity. An interesting speculation would be to attempt to ascertain the character of Campin's and van der Weyden's handwriting. A tendency may be perhaps inferred in Campin's script toward a florid, involved, but always disciplined style. Roger's script appears to be essentially less pictorial and more spiky. A certain conformity points to a lesser degree of phantasy and formal freedom. He also used Gothic script, which, significantly enough, also occurs on the problematic Werl panel.

6.   A similar quality exists, I feel, in the enigmatic group of letters on the vase in the Merode Annunciation. It may have been a cryptogram the meaning of which is now lost but which was intelligible to the circle of "initiated" intellectuals around Campin. We sense a distinct significance in everything he represented; why then would he have belied his nature by placing a string of nonsensical letters in a prominent part of the scene?

Fernand de Mély attempted to decipher the Magdalen inscription. ("Signatures de Primitifs: le rétable de Roger van der Weyden au Louvre et l'inscription du turban de la Madeleine", *Revue Archéologique*, VII, 1918, pp. 50-75). His idea that two groups of letters represent the two Hebrew words Malachah and Kalah, which mean "the art of painting", would be intriguiging if only true. His reading of the following group as "Wiyden" must be rejected because it is composed of Hebrew letters as equally well drawn as in the preceding portion. However, Dr. M. Lutzki from the Jewish Theological Seminary in New York communicated to me that the letters, of which few are misformed, do not make up any Hebrew word. Yet the possibility of a cryptogram remains, a form which seems to have been fancied in the fifteenth century. (Cf. the cryptic device AEIOU of the Austrian Duke Friedrich III from 1444, probably only later interpreted as "Austriae est imperare orbi universe"; or the fanciful way of recording the date in the inscription around the frames of the retable of the Mystical Lamb in

artist's supreme thoroughness in refusing to execute cursorily any motif whatsoever, if this would lead to its being merely approximate or sham; it suggests a man who seeks an integral expression of strength and perfection in every detail he conceives. This is precisely the mode of the cream-white silk brocade of the young man in the Escorial Descent, the pattern of which is almost imperceptible from a distance, and of the remarkable materiality of the body hair on the bare legs of Christ in the same panel and on the Frankfort Thief.

The X-ray photographs show dramatically the profound differences in concept and craftmanship which exist in the five figures and the landscape. They can be explained only by the assumption that they are not all by one artist. Most striking is the difference between the Magdalen and John the Evangelist. The Magdalen shows a masterly sense of volumes, acuteness of expression, formal precision and consummate craftsmanship. The image on the shadowgraph holds its own as an esthetic phenomenon when compared with the painting. We have seen this formal and expressive concordance of the two stages, invisible and visible, so far only in one picture, namely in the portrait of a Woman in the National Gallery in London. The firm yet not severe execution, a continuous and subtle application of the white, which achieves a fine gradation of the light values, and the distinctive shaping of the eyes coincide so closely that I feel that both paintings are by the same artist.[7]

I suggest that this refinement, which has, nevertheless, lost nothing in sureness and monumentality, is characteristic of Campin's last phase of evolution. I do not see any reason to believe that a decline in his art took place but feel rather that he arrived at a refined sublimation and absolute mastery. He would then have been in his early sixties. Why should we picture him as an old man of diminishing artistic powers?[8]

The X-ray picture of the central panel is entirely unlike that of the Magdalen. It catches the painter in the intimacy of his preparatory strokes, gropings and reversals. An impression of a highly strung, less thorough temperament may be gained from the shifting of the shadowy outlines (e.g. the double contour of

Gent). Campin was fond of Hebrew inscriptions painted as if woven into, or embroidered on, fabrics such as on the garment of the soldier in the Resurrection, on the old man's turban in the Entombment in the Seilern triptych, on the inside of the midwife's mantle in the Dijon Nativity, on the shroud in the Louvain Trinity; also on the cuffs, sleeves and collars of figures in the Prado Betrothal. Campin was fairly accurate in the transcription of the letters—unlike Lucas Moser who, in the Tiefenbronn retable, imitated Arabic and Hebrew letters in fanciful inscriptions, disguising the German words, which gave his famous inscription a resigned note.

7 The firmness and concentrated *ductus* of the brushwork of the eyes of the Magdalen, of the London Lady and of Nicodemus from the Escorial are identical.

8 Genius ought not to be measured by the yardstick of normality (and, after all, do the critics expect to find decline or decay in he works of contemporary artists who are in their sixties?)

John's face), the changing of the scheme of the draperies (Mary's veil) and from the general looseness in the definition of the forms. There is a paradoxical discrepancy between the objective precision of the shapes and their modelling in the finished painting and the sketchy, dashing and less disciplined underpainting, which is noticeable mainly in the garments and the landscape. The perfection was attempted only in the upper layers of the painting and was not the artist's concern at the early stage.[9] The paint on the garments was applied with a medium-sized bristle brush, leaving clear marks of nervous strokes. A characteristic feature is that the paint is often brushed across the forms and does not model them attentively during the stroke itself (the eyelids and hair-covering of the Virgin, the eyelids of the Baptist). The impulsive method of working eliminated the need for a precise underdrawing. The X-rays indicate that the painter must have sketched the contours of the folds by impressing lines in the thick wet paint with a dull instrument. This cannot be perceived anywhere on the Magdalen panel. The paint was quite stiff; consequently, all the short brushstrokes on the hands and faces remain clearly visible and, in places, almost produce an effect of hatching with paint (the hands of the Virgin).[10] The contours of the hands are not precise and are devoid of the sculptural quality which distinguishes the bust of the Magdalen. The highlights on John's chalice are recorded with a few quick and determined strokes which reveal the absence of a gradual modelling process. However, the open book of the Baptist received more attention. The landscape in the central panel appears highly cursory in the radiograph, as it is stripped down to vague brushstrokes indicating only the shore line and nothing of the shape of the trees. The stratification of the terrain by means of modulation is absent and the foreground is left without white (although the rock next to John the Evangelist would presumably require some). The rear plane, on the other hand, contains a lot of white. The landscape behind John the Baptist in the left-hand wing is built up more in terms of light, which makes it somewhat akin to the right-hand wing, and yet it is manifestly continuous with the center panel. Trees in the three panels look different and are indeed painted differently. In the left-hand and center panels they are painted in dark, thin paint and thus are almost invisible on the X-ray picture. On the other hand, the trees on the rocks to the right of the Magdalen are underpainted in a dense paint which contains white. We have seen this mode of representation already in the Dijon Nativity. The contrast between the sloppy underpainting in the central panel and the beautiful X-ray reproduction of the landscape behind the Magdalen is significant. Instead of the black emptiness of the former radiograph, here the landscape

9 In terms of psycho-analysis this protean absence of adherence to a firm inner vision of forms may indicate a lack of sincerity and straightforwardness.

10 This recalls the X-ray appearance of the hands of the Man with the Arrow in Brussels.

shows its formation in every detail. The scale of light values is correct and there are no harsh accents; the same phenomenon exists in the figure of the Magdalen.

I feel that the right-hand wing of the Bracque triptych should be attributed to Campin on the basis of comparisons of style and technique with Campin's paintings. The attribution of the entire triptych to one painter is untenable. The problem now remains of reconciling the dating implied from the coat-of-arms of the Bracque couple (certainly not much before 1452) with the life-span of Campin (died 1444). The exterior decoration of the wings is painted by a different, much cruder hand and hence the contemporaneousness of the coat-of-arms with the paintings of the triptych is by no means assured.[11] The possibility exists that the panel with the Magdalen was originally a part of some other work. Thematically she does not belong to the Deesis type portrayed in a variation on the center panel. She is weeping, which is out context with the iconography of the center panel, which shows the victorious Redeemer. The inscription (besides being by a different hand from the others) is not in accord with the character of the four inscriptions. It must be noted that the painting of the Magdalen is much more damaged than the other two panels. In my reconstruction the Magdalen would have been facing a bust of the Man of Sorrows, either in a diptych form (or, less likely, as a triptych with other figures). Campin's diptych would have been broken up and one panel incorporated into a new triptych painted in Roger's studio.[12] The execution of the center panel bears signs of a quick, patched-up commission which did not receive the fullest care. I take the left-hand wing with John the Baptist to be an accomplished work of Roger van der Weyden. On the other hand, the central panel is much weaker, and two figures, i.e. Mary and Christ, are copied from the center of the Beaune polyptych—with a resultant loss in expressive power.[13] Insignificant changes in Mary's figure were made noticeable only in the final layer of the painting; the head-dress and hands in prayer seem to be more similar in their underpainting to the Beaune Virgin. The hands of Christ and of John the Evangelist are below the standard of Roger's art. We suspect

11   The cross and the skull may reflect the meditative leanings of the commissioners but may also point to a dedication by a widow. The latter eventuality would mean that the triptych dates from later than 1452, but it cannot be much later, since Catherine de Brabant soon remarried.

12   Roger may have continued his close relationship with Campin even after he had moved to Brussels. His wife, Elisabeth Goffaert, may have been related to Campin. Beenken, op. cit., p. 12: "die wahrscheinlich eine angeheiratete Nichte des Robert Campins gewesen sein wird."

13   The X-ray photographs are found to be similar, especially those of the head of Christ. Madeleine Hours, "Du polyptyque du Jugement Dernier de l'hôtel-dieu de Beaune", Bulletin du Laboratoire du Musée du Louvre; supplément à la Revue des Arts, Oct. 1957, pp. 22-40, Figs. 11, 12, 14, 15.

either that Roger copied the two figures from his own cartoon with a total dis-
interest or that a helper was perhaps participating in some areas on this panel.

The figure of the Magdalen was preserved in two drawings which are in the
British Museum.[14] It was generally asserted that van der Weyden drew the
better of the two from his own painting. Though remarkably similar to the
painting, I feel that this is rather a preparatory drawing or, at the most, the
artist's copy of the precise underdrawing which may have looked, in its com-
pleteness, like the St. Barbara drawn by Jan van Eyck on a panel. The drawing
could hardly be a copy of the painting. The construction of the body and the
drapery is executed with complete understanding in its double emphasis on the
monumental and sculptural, on the one hand, and the minuteness of a great
realist, on the other, to all of which a copyist could hardly have given complete
expression. The drawing of the eyes is even more expressive than in the painting. The absence of the Hebrew inscription on the hat and of the brocade
pattern on the drawing, as well as the more markedly emphasized tectonic
quality of the folds, leads me to think that it is rather a preparatory drawing.

The outlines are emphasized but never wiry. The strong and bold lines
always seek the maximum expression of the bulk and volume, which they
define admirably.[15] The modelling with long, disciplined lines in the garments
and more minute ones in the face, as well as the very robust quality of the line,
coincides with the drawing of the Good Thief by Campin in the Fogg Art
Museum at Harvard University.[16] Strength and sensitivity are combined here
in the work of a great talent. In the light of this striking similarity, I believe
that the drawing of the Magdalen is also by Campin and separated from the
drawing in the Fogg Museum by less than ten years. The common authorship
of the two drawings is indirect evidence for the attribution of the panel with
St. Magdalen to Robert Campin. I submit that Campin's art of drawing, besides
the underdrawing revealed by the infra-red rays, is made known to us in these
two masterly drawings.

14   The second drawing is clearly a later copy. Jules Destrée, *Roger de la Pasture*
(Paris, 1930), Pl. 105B-D.

15   This is far removed from the point of view of Roger. I see his personal style
rather in the drawing of a woman in the British Museum. Beenken, *op. cit.*, Fig. 27.

16   The similarity had already been acknowledged by Jakob Rosenberg, "A Silver-
point Drawing by the Master of Flémalle Acquired by the Fogg Art Museum", *The Art
Quarterly*, 13, 1950, p. 250 f.

Conclusion

I have attempted in the series of analyses of Campin's paintings to single out the essential character and uniqueness of his art. In order to arrive at a sublimation of his style I have sought vigorously to recognize and to remove all alien incrustations—i.e. attributions which have been painted in a different spirit and portions of his paintings which have been added by another hand—which disfigured his artistic profile. The discovery of the basic and true features of Campin's style and its range had thus made it possible to enlarge his *oeuvre* by several new attributions. The chief among them, the Escorial Descent, makes his name shine even more brightly with the dazzling light of a star of the first order. He and van Eyck were the creators of new Flemish painting.

The most intriguing problem of this period is the enigmatic artistic symbiosis of Campin and van der Weyden—each a great artist in his own right —whose activities approached each other and ran parallel in a curious way. It therefore gave rise to the theory that they were identical. This is, of course, impossible, as we are confronted with two distinct sets of works imbued with different aims and ideals—works of two different temperaments. Campin's characterization, together with that of one (or two) anonymous collaborator(s), has been set forth on the previous pages and finally contrasted with van der Weyden's. It would thus be superfluous to describe their personalities here in my own words. I prefer therefore to quote Paul Jamot, who characterized admirably the essence of the two concepts of art.[1]

1 *Op. cit.*, p. 268. The task of studying critically all attributions to van der Weyden is an important project, waiting to be undertaken.

"D'un côté un dessin puissant, vigoureux, qui cherche l'expression et le caractère, plus que la grâce, dans les types de la grandeur, de la dignité, du pathétique, un sentiment sculptural du relief comme on en a peu vu au cours de toute l'histoire ... le même idéal de sculpteur dans la composition, serée, massée et pourtant claire, aux contours nets et géometriques, idéal qu'accuse encore le fond d'or sur lequel se détachent les figures.

De l'autre côté, une certaine banalité dans les types plus de qualités aimables que de force, une habileté de décorateur que l'on ne peut nier mais une composition qui est toute contraire aux principes et aux vertus de la sculpture, composition assez lâche et dispersée, avec des vides peu calculés, qui rapelle plutôt, malgré les dimensions de l'œuvre, le métier du miniaturiste. Or, il s'agit là d'oppositions fondamentales."

Paul Jamot wrote this apt characterization with a different purpose in mind. He was led to believe that Campin's paintings were nothing more than a phase in van der Weyden's production. He chose to cull the essence of Roger's art from the Escorial Descent, without doubt the most perfect and magnificent of the paintings ascribed to Roger. He contrasted it with another characterization which he distilled from a contemplation of the Beaune polyptych and assumed that it was painted by an artist other than Roger. He grasped admirably the differences of the two in his qualitative appraisal, with which I fully agree. I only differ with him in respect of the actual persons hinged to the two kinds of art defined. In connoisseurship the lucid recognition of an artistic personality is far more important, as it makes it possible to associate with the key monument other paintings pervaded with the same spirit. Jamot did, in fact, attach van der Weyden's name to Campin's work whilst discovering the true characteristics of his style; however, in doing this, he made orphans of a group of paintings of a highly personal style, which differ fundamentally from the Descent style—and these are genuine works of Roger. Their style is, in fact, that of the Beaune altarpiece. Perhaps it is not quite fair to use the latter as a touchstone of Roger's genius, since assistants collaborated on the large ensemble. In concept, however, it was the brain-child of Roger, and about this there can be no doubt. It was on this basis and not on the actual execution that the polyptych was appraised by Jamot. The very words he uses fully apply to the paintings which, I believe, epitomize the qualities and artistic endeavor of Roger—namely, the Vienna Crucifixion triptych, the Granada altarpiece of the Virgin, the Uffizi Entombment, the Bladelin and Columba altarpieces, Pietàs in the Prado and London National Gallery and a number of portraits.

Roger van der Weyden was a successful and celebrated artist (yet it is not always exclusively on greatness and originality of spirit that the purple raiment of fame is bestowed). There is no doubt that he was a painter of great significance who shaped his creations with remarkable intellectual power, for two ensuing generations zealously embraced the style of this great eclectic. Yet he was also a practical, cool (despite all spiritual piety), mannered and elegant spirit who never permitted his imagination to be inflamed by an exciting array of sparkling colors, embellishing powerful forms which he instinctively avoided. It is to the taciturn image of Robert Campin that the titanic greatness belongs. In the impenetrable twilight we discern the tragic dichotomy of an undisciplined life and a highly disciplined and grandiose art. Yet his monumental style did not have a dominant effect on the further course of Flemish art: he and the van Eycks were of the same race of artists whose style was too intensely personal to sire a school. The advanced vision of the world and the difficulties involved in imitating a technique inseparably bound up with concept were formidable obstacles for the average painters. Nevertheless, Campin's style affected Flemish painting indirectly through the art of his pupil, Roger, who incorporated Campin's elements in his own milder, less exceptional idiom. Campin's awe-inspiring, monumental and strongly sculptural form of expression prevented his from being a prophet in his own country.[2] The Netherlands of the progressing fifteenth and early sixteenth centuries sought in paintings other values such as finiteness, regularity, gentleness of mood, finesse, elegance and a pleasing gamut of color.

2   It seems that a few contemporary German painters communicated better with his forceful vision of forms but paraphrazed them more crudely as they were rooted in an autochtonous and more archaic tradition (Witz, Multscher, Moser, Lochner; in Austria, the Master of the Albrecht Altarpiece).

Appendix

The question of copies is closely related to the question of Campin's style and has been touched upon in a few instances on the preceding pages. I am not so much concerned here with later copies since they usually give us only a glimpse of the master's composition at the most and they do not supply any reliable information neither on the morphology nor his technique.[1]

Let us first mention a small Crucifixion panel in the Musée Royal d'Art Ancien in Brussels. It is labeled: "Ecole des Anciens Pays-Bas", first half of the XV. century. The panel is obviously a fragment and a substantial part of the surface is repainted.[2] The figure of Christ has a more archaic character

---

1 Examples of this are the Vengeance of Tomyris and the Adoration of the Magi in the Berlin-Dahlem Museum, Colin de Coter's St. Luke Painting the Virgin in the church in Vieure, Gerard David's Crucifixion in the Thyssen Collection in Lugano, The Virgin with St. Joseph in Le Puy, and the drawing of Jael Slaying Sisera in the Braunschweig Landesmuseum (Panofsky, *op. cit.*, pls. 104-105). Some Flémallesque elements exist in the wings by a German painter, Ammann von Ravensburg divided between the Galleria Estense de Modena, University Library in Liège, and Museo Correr in Venice (Nativity of the Virgin, Annunciation, Visitation, SS. Margaret, Dorothea, Catherine and Barbara, all 75 x 31 cm). Friedrich Winkler, "Ein deutsch-niederländischer Altar in Oberitalien", *Zeitschrift für Kunstwissenschaft*, 1947-48, Figs. 2 and 3, and "Jos Ammann von Ravensburg", *Jahrbuch der Berliner Museen* (Jahrbuch der Preussischen Kunstsammlungen N.F.), 1959, pp. 51-118.

2 The grain of the portion of wood added at the bottom runs horizontally while the panel itself has a vertical grain. The X-rays show by revealing a portion of large scroll

than the three angels holding the symbols of the Passion; they could hardly have been painted by one and the same painter's hand. It is helpful that there exist two panels on which the entire composition is represented: the complete figures of the angels have inscription scrolls about them and the large lower part is occupied in an Intercession scene, by the figures of Mary and a donor with empty scrolls against a brocaded wall. The copy in the museum of St. Salvator's church in Bruges is still from the XV century while the other in the Museo Galdiano in Madrid belongs to the XVI century. In this case a lady is represented instead.

The X-ray photograph is interesting as it reveals differences from the present appearance. The lower right angel was originally painted from the profile and the body of Christ was thinner and constructed in a different way which is very remarkable in His head. Its style and that of the angel at the left as revealed by the X-rays belong to the pre-Eyckian painting.[3]

On the other hand the present body conforms to the style of Campin's bodies in the earlier stage of his evolution while the head can be compared with Christ in the Prado Descent. Christ is represented frontally and lacks typical Rogerian features which influenced much of the subsequent Flemish painting, such as the swinging of the flexed knees to the side and elegantly fluttering loincloth.

The body is painted in impasto which is finer and more enamel-like on the face, as the details called for a greater precision. Some forms still do not attain a fully naturalistic rendering (knees, calves) and the bodily conformation is reminiscent of the forms in the early Seilern triptych. The greenish tones in the shading of the face would also point to an early stage of Campin's evolution. The chest and abdomen are already painted with a considerable sense of anatomy. Christ's head is modelled with a great sensitivity and feeling for a pathos of expression. The large back part of the head (which, by the way, is a distinguishing feature of the Byzantine Christs) is similarly shaped to that of the Bad Thief in Frankfort. (In any case, the Crucifixion in Berlin which is as-

---

and other unclear shapes that it is a part of the same panel, probably taken from its original lower right edge. Moreover, several demon-like heads may be recognized at the left.

3   This archaic, strictly frontal representation of the straight hanging body of Christ was also used in the Crucifixion in the Milan-Turin Hours (Turin, Museo Civico), in an Eyckian Calvary in Berlin and by an imitator of Campin in another Calvary in the same museum. (A detailed notation of anatomical forms in the last panel shows that it could not be contemporary with Campin.) This early type remained for long popular with German artists (Grünewald) while in Flanders it was largely supplanted with a less hieratic, freer posture traceable to van der Weyden's prototypes. The style, technique and coloring of the angels clad in yellow-orangy robes are entirely different from Christ. The scroll bears a gold inscription: Consummatum est. A similarly placed scroll appears, e.g., in the just mentioned pastiche Calvary in Berlin (Panofsky, op. cit., fig. 398).

signed to the Campin's circle, appears to be more removed from Campin's prototypes.) The entire figure in the Brussels picture produces the strong sculptural effect which is a salient feature of Campin's art. Perhaps in this painting we have an information how did look Campin's Christ on the Cross since we may suppose that the Calvary did not miss in the repertory of his work. I suggest the possibility, in view of its quality and style, that this fragment is directly associated with Campin's studio. The re-using of an older painted panel is not unique in the Campin's circle: it has been noticed in the Reading Magdalen in the National Gallery in London.

Of the reliable copies of works from Campin's early period the type of the Madonna in an Apse, which exists in a number of replicas, and the Trinity in the Museum Van der Kelen-Mertens in Louvain should be mentioned first. The typology, drapery and technique in the best of the Madonna's copies (The Metropolitan Museum of Art and Weizner Gallery in New York)[4] and in the Trinity panel have an archaic spirit, which indicate that they may have been painted within the lifetime of Campin. Both reflect the early style of Campin and many comparisons may be made between the angel's faces and those in the Seilern and Dijon paintings.

The Louvain Trinity gives likewise a fair picture of the master's style. The principle of closely packed relief is here most strongly expressed and would point to the origin of its model in the time of the Merode retable. A study of the technique establishes convincingly that it is not from the hand of Campin, for, to give an example, the pattern of the weave on the shroud is painted over the Hebrew inscription, which is contrary to the master's judiciously factual approach. Infra-red photography shows an approximate, sketchy underdrawing very much different from that in the Merode Annunciation. The copyist, however, obviously did not trace the forms in his sketch exactly as they were placed in the original. His approach was quite free, since the underdrawing deviates considerably from the final placing of several details (such as God's hand, Christ's feet, the lower right-hand angel's face, etc.); yet the composition definitely remained in the spirit of Campin. The paint of the flesh is thick and

4 Further very similar copies are in Sarasota, Ringling Museum of Art, in the Gendebien Collection in Brussels and in the London National Gallery. More distant copies are in the Joly collection in Brussels, one sold at Sotheby's in London in 1962, in Berlin, in Lisbon, Museu Nacional de Arte Antigua, in Zagreb, Museum Umjetnosti, in Philadelphia, Johnson Collection, in the Toledo Museum of Art. The two angels are omitted in a variant of the composition (the museum in Oldenburg and Statens Museum för Konst in Copenhagen) or are moved on to the wings (Collection Hernalsteen-Van der Waarden in Brussels and in 1929 Sotheby's Sale in London). The Virgin's type persisted into the XVI century, mostly in the Spanish examples but the absidial setting was dropped in favor of Manneristic columnar architecture or open landscape (collections Homar, Muntadas and Amatller in Barcelona, in the Prado in Madrid, in Cadiz, Museo Provincial, in Poznan, Muzeum Narodowe and in the monastery of Pedralbet near Barcelona).

the modelling is of an umber color and the eyelids, eyebrows and nostrils are drawn with sepia or greenish umber. A very similar type of shading exists in a Portrait of a Lady in the National Gallery in London and in the large Cruci-fixion diptych in the Philadelphia Museum of Art and the Man of Sorrows in the Municipal Museum in Bruges, attributed to van der Weyden. These attri-butions seem to me questionable from the standpoint of technique and quality.[5]

The lost prototype of the Trinity was later copied in a somewhat enlarged version by Colin de Coter (Louvre).[6] He followed the original more closely in some respects (e.g. the feet are placed higher). A panel in the Louvre forming the right wing to the Trinity panel proudly bears an inscription on the hem of the half-kneeling Magdalen (?) : Colin de Coter pingit me in Brabancia, Bruselle. The subject is the three Sorrowing Marys, the youngest of whom— and the one most prominently placed—may be taken as a disguised likeness of the donatress or the wife of the donor, who would have been represented, also in a kneeling position of adoration, on the lost left-hand wing. What interests us here is that Coter must have copied Campin's original even in the Marys' wing, which gives us an idea of the appearance of the original triptych. The composition is very Campinesque—built up in a high relief manner, in which the eloquence of powerful shapes is not disturbed by any awkward overlap-ping. The physiognomies themselves, even though remolded in Coter's trans-position of the original, still preserve much of Champin's types, and the drapery retains its original opulence; the voluminous expansive garment of the Magdalen was, of course, modernized by Coter.[7]

The Prado Annunciation is, in my opinion, a copy of Campin's original com-position rather than a mere pastiche on his style. The argument about the

---

5   This tentative grouping will require further investigation before it could be pro-posed as such. Their author would then perhaps emerge as a painter who was active making replicas of the master's works first in Campin's, then in van der Weyden's studios.

6   167 x 118 cm as compared to 124,5 x 90 cm of the Louvain panel. Infra-red photo-graphs of both copies are reproduced by J. Taubert, op. cit., pp. 22, 26, 31. A Trinity embroidered on a vestment for the high Mass of the Order of the Golden Fleece in the Schatzkammer in Vienna shows that Campin's scheme was adopted by Roger's studio as the type of Christ's head suggests (Bauch, op. cit., fig. 8). Campin's composition served as a basis for several later paintings such as in the Brussels Museum of Ancient Art and in Cologne, Wallraf-Richartz Museum.

7   It may even be speculated that her clasped hands represent the original configura-tion of this motif by Campin and that this very gesture was also planned originally by Campin for his Magdalen in the Escorial Descent. Its solidity, monumentality and forth-rightness would better match the resigned grieving mood of Nicodemus than her mannered wringing of her hands in Roger's rendering. De Coter did us a good service because he copied still other paintings of Campin, now lost, and preserved thus their likeness. It is a Descent from the Cross in Stuttgart, Museum der bildenden Kunst (No. 741), and St. Luke Painting the Virgin in the church in Vieure.

un-Campinesque iconography of the Annunciation taking place in a church interior is not fully convincing. On the contrary, some highly realistic touches, such as the triumphal arch walled-in with red bricks, the houses appearing above the open-work parapet at the top and the trees in the church garden, are related to the spirit and representational interests of Campin. The coarser quality of execution does not measure up to the level of the master's art. Another of the paintings attributed to the school of Campin, the Mass of St. Gregory, known from two replicas, is also a copy harking back to Campin's prototype.[8] The figures of Christ and the kneeling acolyte point to an early phase not far removed from the Seilern triptych.

The panel with the half-figures of Christ and Mary in the Johnson Collection in the Philadelphia Museum of Art is an uninspired copy after the master. The X-ray photograph of Mary's face shows a technique totally different from Campin.[9] The fingers of Christ's left hand, crowded at the bottom into the scene, tend to contradict the assumption that it is a fragmentarily preserved panel.

A type of the bust of the Virgin with the Child in a tondo form, small in size, which is believed to have been created by Campin, became evidently popular. It exists in some ten copies, more or less close one to each other. It seems that these little pictures were suspended on the canopy in the heads of the conjugal beds. The prototype is lost but the master's style may be recognized in the facial types and the drapery which may be compared, for example, with the Frankfort Virgin; yet an occasional awkwardness (Mary's ear, Child's left hand) betrays the copyist.[10]

To the contrary, in the Annunciation in the Brussels museum one gets the feeling that this is a more ambitious and freer replica of the Merode Annunciation by a contemporary of Campin. The types have some amount of independence about them and some accessories are likely due to the imagination of the painter himself. Two faithful copies of the Merode version are extant (Kassel,

8 The copy, formerly in E. Schwarz Coll., now in Acquavella Gallery in New York is reproduced in Panofsky, *op. cit.*, fig. 227. The other copy is in the Musée Royal in Brussels.

9 Burroughs' article in the *Metropolitan Museum Studies*, loc. cit., figs. 10 and 18. A large part of Christ's face is reconstructed.

10 One was recently published by Leo van Puyvelde, "A Tondo of the Time of the Van Eycks", *The Art Quarterly*, Autumn 1961, pp. 259-61. Such tondos exist in the museum in Barcelona (perhaps the best among the replicas), in the museum in Brussels, in the Landesmuseum in Hannover, in Antwerp, Coll. Marshall, in Philadelphia, Johnson Coll., in Baltimore, Walters Art Gallery. Inferior are those in Dijon (museum), in Antwerp, coll. Simkers, Wildenstein Gallery in New York and in Leipzig, coll. Fritz von Hanck. Their sizes vary between less than 20 to less than 30 cm and the frame is usually part of the panel itself. In two cases Latin invocations of the Virgin run around the periphery of the panels—Ave Maria celorum mater regis angelorum (museum in Brussels) and Ave mater dei ora pro nobis nunc et in ... (Leipzig).

Genova) as it was mentioned in the section dealing with the Merode triptych.

The large panel with a Madonna with Saints in the Enclosed Garden in the National Gallery in Washington presents several problems.[11] The facial types, hands and drapery style are inspired by Campin's work but the brushwork is not identical; therefore, only his assistant can be considered as the author. An impersonal smoothness and unpleasant slickness of the flesh parts painted in pink with greenish-gray shading contrasts oddly with the more daring execution of the garments. Moreover, some anatomical details, such as the veins on John the Baptist's legs and the lower eyelids of Catherine, are just cursory additions not organically integrated into the brushwork rendering the forms. The colors are generally duller and, with the exception of the pink of Catherine's mantle, lack the strength and sparkling quality of Campin's originals. The lack of a daring color harmony is especially noticeable on John the Baptist and the surrounding area. The lower left corner is, however, by a more distinguished hand, as can be seen in St. Catherine's mantle, the sword, the wheel, the iris.

Closest of all to Campin's types is the Christ Child (cf. the Child in Frankfort), while Mary and Catherine recall strongly the types of Mary and the angel in the Brussels Annunciation, so that the two panels must be linked. The countenance of John the Baptist and Anthony the Hermit lack the expressive energy intrinsic in Campin's men; they are the weakest in the composition.

The reading of the X-ray negatives is diffucult owing to the presence of a cradling and flake-white which fills the grain of the oak panel. It shows a technique and brushwork unrelated to Campin. Some faces (Barbara and Catherine) were modelled with a dense paint containing white. The male heads lack totally firm underpainting, as all the modelling was done in the upper semi-glaze layer. Still the closest to Campin's method, though insensitive in the shaping of the nose, appear to be the heads of St. Barbara and the Child. Some similarity to the X-ray appearance of Daret's paintings may be detected.[12] The hands and legs have approximate, hazy contours and the density of white underpainting varies considerably, so that some hands are invisible. On the other hand, the draperies are firmly traced. Few *pentimenti* may be detected in Catherine's mantle and in John's hand.

There are several portraits allegedly copied from Campin's originals. It is plausible to recognize the characteristics of Campin's earlier style in the copies of a pair of portraits—of Bartholomé Alatruy and Marie de Pacy in the Museum in Tournai [13] and in a portrait of a man in a red headdress in Berlin-Dahlem

11   No. 1388. *Catalogue of the Paintings and Sculptures from the Kress Collection,* 1951, p. 168, 120 cm high. Called: The Master of Flémalle and Assistants. According to J. D. Passavant (1833), the panel was formerly in a church in Bruges.

12   Burroughs, *op. cit.,* Fig. 90.

13   Von Tschudi, *op. cit.,* p. 100 f. Oblique reflected light shows that the portraits were painted over some thickly painted shapes (heraldic designs?). X-rays would bring a more specific information.

(No. 587). The portrait of a Princess in Dumbarton Oaks, Washington, belongs also to the orbit of Campin's early style but the linearism is too pronounced.[14] On the other hand, the Portrait of a Musician in New York, Mrs. J. Magnin Collection, can hardly be connected with Campin because of the failure to keep the various parts of the face united in one homogeneous and convincing spherical volume.[15]

The beginnings of this objective trend are difficult to visualize in the absence of a proper criterion. The profile portrait of Wenceslaus of Luxemburg in the Thyssen Collection in Lugano may be perhaps connected with this early Flemish production, as the well expressed corporality, the interest in light and shade and the bold brushwork would suggest.[16]

Finally, a few observations may be made on the kinship of some paintings, with the aim of ascertaining whether they can be grouped together and whether in such a group a development of some single hand may be recognized. This procedure of the grouping of paintings many of which paraphrase the art of Campin and van der Weyden may eventually lead to the establishing of a corpus of works by a few anonymus painters who worked in the shadow of the great masters. They very probably will remain anonymous, at least until the entire production is thoroughly sifted and some chance evidence for their identification is found. Some of them were almost as skilful technicians as the masters, which makes it doubly difficult to be sure of the attributions. When confronted with two identical compositions of high quality execution, the art critics readily concede that one of them is a replica of an expert, perhaps even contemporary, copyist (e.g. the triptych of John the Baptist, the Granada retable, St. Luke Painting the Virgin, portrait of Robert de Masmines). The solution of the problem is rationally feasible, as both materials for comparison are extant. But often is does not occur to them that such a skilled painter might have been able to paint compositions in his own right, strongly dependent, but still very good. The critics prefer to call these works, in the absence of exact comparisons (as they were not copies), by the names of the famous artists. There is therefore an implicit danger that any excellent preserved copies might

14   Panofsky, *op. cit.*, Fig. 221.
15   *Ibid.*, Fig. 219.
16   Rudolf J. Heinemann, *Sammlung Schloss Rohoncz*, 1958. No. 142a, Pl. 90. It is interesting to note that a newly discovered painting in Berlin, representing the half-figure of a Madonna with angels, contains germs of Campin's style in the types of the Child and of the lower angels and in the concept of objective realism (rendering of the lace). The four uppermost angels seem to be by a different and inferior painter. This painting may perhaps throw some light on the problem of Campin's artistic formation. The picture, painted on canvas (107 x 81 cm), shows Flemish rather than French strain. Friedrich Winkler, "Ein frühfranzösisches Marienbild", *Jahrbuch der Berliner Museen*, I, 1959, pp. 179-189. Millard Meiss and Colin Eisler, "A New French Primitive", *The Burlington Magazine*, June 1960, pp. 233-240.

also be attributed to the master, if the original model is lost, although the existence of fellow painters who attained technical excellence cannot be denied.

A nucleus of one group may be formed by two paintings which are united by a common style, typology and brushwork, that is the Madonna Seated on a Lawn (Berlin) and the Brussels Annunciation of the Merode type. The Madonna, the earlier of the two, belongs to the stratum of the stylistic evolution exemplified by the Seilern triptych and her typology may well be compared with the faces of a couple of angels singled out in the discussion of that triptych. They lack the intense realistic interest pervading Campin's paintings. The formal and iconographical treatment of the two panels establishes that their author was very close to Campin in the twenties. He might have been working along with Campin even before, if we recognize the previously discussed portions, which were added to the paintings of the Seilern triptych, as being from his hand.

By comparing these works with the four panels which adorned the wings of a sculptured shrine commissioned in 1434 by Jean du Clerq, Abbot of St. Vaast in Arras, and completed in July 1435, close mutual links are revealed, which may perhaps signify a common authorship. The following panels were recognized by Hulin de Loo as once having composed the Arras retable: The Visitation (Berlin), Nativity (Thyssen, Lugano), Epiphany (Berlin) and Presentation in the Temple (Paris). A similarity as between feminine types in the Arras panels, the above-mentioned panels and the Leningrad and Aix Madonnas suggests with some degree of probability that Jacques Daret was the author of the whole group (e.g. Mary in the Arras Visitation and the Brussels Annunciation, the minuteness of the hands and a peculiar weak gesture of Mary in the Annunciation and of an old woman on the right in the Presentation as well in the Berlin and Leningrad Virgins). The chief feature of the Annunciation in Brussels and the Nativity in Lugano is that they are free replicas of Campin's compositions. Daret during his many years in Campin's atelier had a chance to become thoroughly acquainted with the paintings of his master and perhaps even collaborated in some. The Berlin Madonna and the Annunciation followed by the Virgin with Saints in Washington may be still from the time of his apparenticeship, while the Leningrad and Aix Madonnas represent a mature stage in the career of the painter whom I tentatively propose to indentify as Daret.[17] The representation of Christchild in Berlin and Leningrad may well be

17   The complexity of the problem of the group of paintings executed by the *alter ego*—or perhaps a *tertius ego* of Campin—may be illustrated by calling attention to the spirit of the minuscule pervading all the forms in the Aix panel on the one side and the Medici Madonna in Frankfort on the other side. The heads of St. Peter in both works may be compared. One may perhaps go further with the comparison and juxtapose the proportional narrowness of the doctor-saint in the Medici panel, the kneeling donor Oberto (?) de Villa on the left-hand wing of the triptych in the Abegg Collection in

compared. The drapery style with its deep furrows and the narrow ridges of the folds in the Leningrad Madonna and the Werl panels seems to be an improved and evolved version of the style already existing in the Brussels Annunciation. To this tentative chain may be added the large panel with the Virgin and Saints in Washington and the portrait of a man in a red headgear in Berlin.

A drawing of a *Sacra conversazione* in the Louvre shows the same type of Mary face as that used by Daret.[18] The sharp, slightly Semitic features apparent in Daret's Arras retable appear in the face of Elizabeth in the Visitation in the Galleria Sabauda in Turin. The latter has the qualities of mature works in its special construction. It should be noted that the Turin Visitation more clearly embodies the principles of the art of Campin than those of van der Weyden, recognition of which might be useful for its classification; likewise the brushwork, revealed by the X-rays, is unlike that I have pointed out as typical of Roger. On the other hand, Roger's characteristics are prominent in the Visitation in the Speck von Sternburg Collection in Lützschena; here there is more aloofness and spirituality in the countenances, but also much less tectonic logic in the construction and postures. The typical Rogerian flatness and linear quality forces the perspective of the castle to be less correct than the accomplished perspective in the Turin Visitation. The more intense realism and the greater sculptural and dramatic qualities of the Turin panel show the author to be a follower of Campin rather than of van der Weyden. This presumption makes the Annunciation in the Louvre a problem, as this is usually attributed to van der Weyden. It was recognized that the Annunciation formed the center of a triptych of which the wings were the Visitation and a partly repainted donor's panel in Turin. Why is it that characteristics of the two great painters are both present in this dismembered retable? Maybe the Flemish Parnassus had more talented painters than is usually realised. It should be stated in addition that Daret was, as I suspect, primarily a competitor of Roger van der Weyden and apparently quite open to influences, his attitude to his own work being therefore

---

Zug and a beggar in the background of the Presentation in the Columba altarpiece in Munich. (Beenken, *op. cit.*, Figs. 53, 102, 116). There is also a certain "tininess" about the head of Canon Werl in the Prado. The linking of the paintings on the basis of a certain congeniality by no means implies a common authorship. It merely indicates the possible work of eclectic imitators possessing great skill who worked on their own or occasionally collaborated with the masters. It is known that Canon Werl in 1435 travelled with Cardinal Albergati through Tournai to Arras where they had the change to admire the altarpiece which had recently been painted by Jacques Daret for the Abbey of St. Vaast. (Pieper, *op. cit.*, p. 93 f.) It is tempting to conjecture that Werl, being impressed with Daret's paintings, commissioned from him the retable which bears the dedication date 1438. This would still not make the participation of Campin impossible (St. Barbara) if one considers that he was barred from concluding contracts officially.

18   Panofsky, *op. cit.*, Fig. 231.

like that described by Molière when he said: "Je prends mon bien où je le trouve." [19]

The purpose of this Appendix has been to list a few rough observations which may possibly serve as an incentive for further investigation. A critical appraisal of replicas is a difficult field, as the individual personality is often deliberately submerged or suppressed in the process of copying. The grouping of paintings according to their innate execution and psychological qualities is a reasonable proposition and can cause a surprising amount of reshuffling to take place. One of the tasks is to follow up the work of Jacques Daret.[20] We know nothing of his mature and late styles and there has been no serious attempt to extend the evolution of his art, in a continuous line of works which could be attributed to him beyond the Arras altar shrine.[21] His personality has always been used in works of criticism as the convenient contrast of a "feeble and unimaginative painter" to the creative genius of Campin and van der Weyden. Yet it seems to me that the criticism is based on the works of a young painter who was at that time in his late twenties and was not so bad a painter for that age, although certainly not a genius (see his Visitation in Berlin and the Nativity in Lugano). It was his misfortune to live at the same time and the same place as these great masters and thus his talent inevitably fades in the presence of their art. He—and Petrus Christus, for that matter— in different historical circumstances would have been evaluated with a less scornful eye, if they had lived in any country other than the brilliant Netherlands of the fifteenth century. On

19   There are some other works of considerable quality, which vacillate in their inspiration between Campin's and van der Weyden's styles, such as a Madonna of Humility formerly in the collection of G. Müller in Brussels now in Baronne Gendebien Collection in Brussels. (Panofsky, Fig. 226), which is not unlike the Medici Madonna in Frankfort, and a similar iconographical scene of a Madonna on a Crescent in the Municipal Museum in Douai and in Brussels, Collection Comte de Jonghe, (Ruth Massey Tovell, *Roger van der Weyden and the Flémalle Enigma*, Toronto 1955, p. 5). The Child, slender in bodily proportions, is quite like those in the "Group Daret". In this respect relationship exists to the painting in Aix-en-Provence. Weaker copies exist in Cologne, Wallraf-Richartz Museum and in Madrid, coll. of Duke of Infantado.
20   Yet another elusive task would be to study the hypothetical work of Daniel Daret, his half-brother and pupil, who became a court painter to the Duke of Burgundy in 1446, in succession to Jan van Eyck. It can be presumed that he was more than a mediocre painter. After exploring all the possible avenues, as a result of the indispensable scepticism of the reseacher, one begins to wonder if Daniel's art was not linked with Campin's in a more intimate manner rather than just through the intermediary of Jacques. Let us remember that Campin was no longer able legally to have any pupils after his conviction in 1429, but still he could have trained the brother of his pupil of many years.
21   Carla Gottlieb, *op. cit.,* argues in favor of Daret's authorship of the Brussels Annunciation, which has already been suggested by Burroughs. It would still fall into his early period.

the other hand, this customary form of negative appraisal is justified to some degree, because his art, without the illustrious models, could never have reached the niveau which it attained. I think that an objective apparaisal must be written in a monograph on Daret (or, perhaps, the two Darets) and a re-examination of the problems suggested in the Appendix as a mere outline may be useful for this task.

Plates

Figs. 1–3. Entombbment Triptych, Count Antoine Seilern, London. Center 60 × 48.9 cm, wings 60 × 22.5 cm.

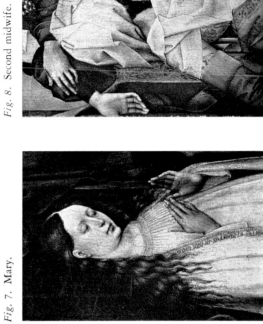

Fig. 6. One midwife.

Fig. 8. Second midwife.

Details of the Dijon Nativity

Fig. 5. Joseph.

Fig. 7. Mary.

Fig. 4. The Nativity, Musée de Dijon. 87 × 70 cm.

Fig. 9. Virgin and Child, National Gallery, London. 63,5 × 49 cm.

Fig. 10. Virgin and Child, X-ray *photograph.*

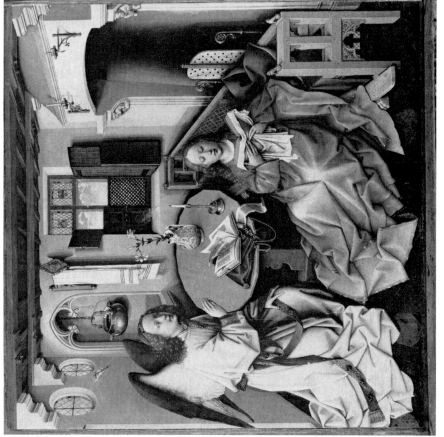

Figs. 11–13. Annunciation (Merode) Triptych, The Cloisters, The Metropolitan Museum of Art, New York. Center 62,5 × 62 cm, wings 62,5 × 26,3 cm.

Fig. 14. Head of the donor, *Infra-red photograph.*   *Fig. 15.* Detail of the angel, *Infra-red photograph.*

Details of the Merode Triptych

Fig. 16. Head of the angel.   *Fig. 17.* Head of the Virgin.

Fig. 20. The gatehouse in the donors' wing. *Infra-red photograph.*

Fig. 19. Donors' wing, (lower part), *X-ray photograph.*

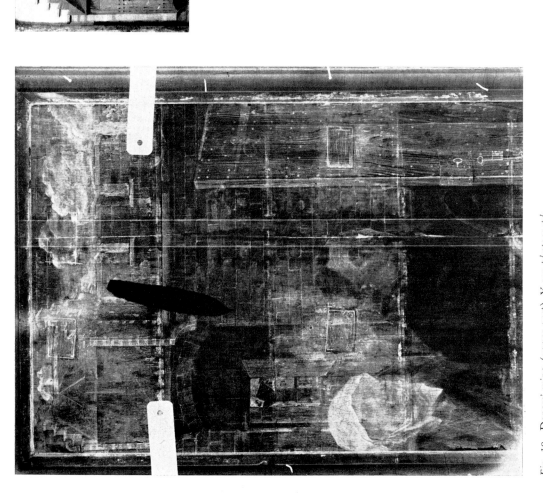

Fig. 18. Donors' wing (upper part) *X-ray photograph.*

Details of the Merode Triptych

Fig. 21. The angel, *X-ray-photograph.*

Fig. 22. The Virgin, *X-ray photograph.*

Details of the Merode Triptych

Fig. 24. St. Joseph, *X-ray photograph.*

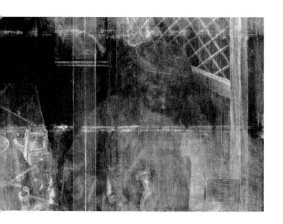

Fig. 23. Head of Joseph.

Fig. 25. Virgin and Child, Städelsches Kunstinstitut, Frankfurt. 159 × 68,5 cm.

Fig. 26. St. Veronica, Städelsches Kunstinstitut, Frankfurt. 155 × 61 cm.

Fig. 29. The Trinity, Städelsches Kunstinstitut, Frankfurt. 148,7 × 61 cm.

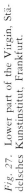

Fig. 27. Lower part of the Virgin, Städelsches Kunstinstitut, Frankfurt.

Fig. 28. Lower part of St. Veronica, Städelsches Kunstinstitut, Frankfurt.

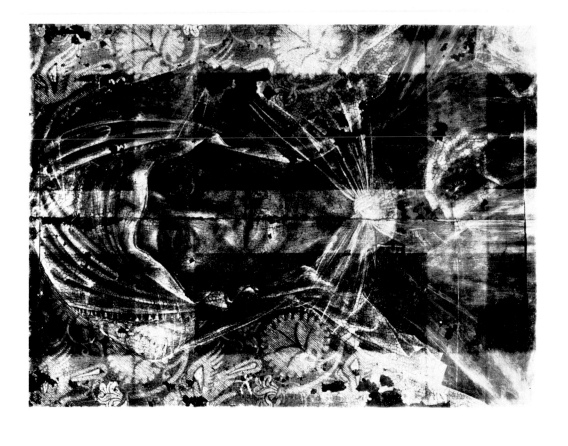

Fig. 31. Upper part of St. Veronica. Städelsches Kunstinstitut, Frankfurt, *X-ray photograph.*

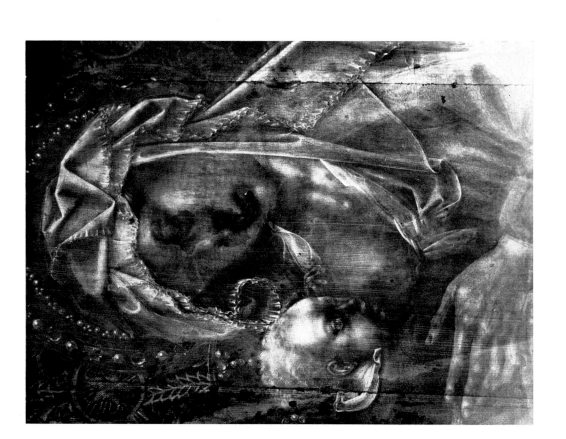

Fig. 30. Upper part of the Virgin and Child, Städelsches Kunstinstitut, Frankfurt, *X-ray photograph.*

Fig. 33. Good(?) Thief on the Cross, Städelsches Kunstinstitut, Frankfurt. 133 × 92,5 cm.

Fig. 32. Drawing of the Bad(?) Thief on the Cross, Fogg Art Museum, Cambridge, 17,5 × 9,8 cm.

Fig. 34. Mater Dolorosa (reverse of the panel with the Virgin and Child) Städelsches Kunstinstitut, Frankfurt.

Fig. 35. Upper part of the Virgin and Child, Städelsches Kunstinstitut.

Fig. 37. Portrait of a Woman, National Gallery, London, *X-ray photograph.*

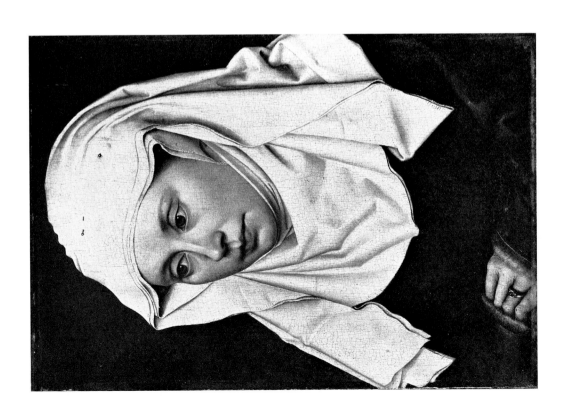

Fig. 36. Portrait of a Woman, National Gallery, London, 40.7 × 27 cm.

Fig. 39. Portrait of a Stout Man, Thyssen Collection, Lugano, *X-ray photograph.*

Fig. 38. Portrait of a Stout Man, Thyssen Collection, Lugano. 35 × 24 cm.

Descent from the Cross, Museo de Prado, Madrid. 202 × 260 cm.

Fig. 41. Young Man and Joseph of Arimathia, Museo de Prado, Madrid.

Fig. 42. Head of Nicodemus.

Fig. 43. Head of the Virgin.

Fig. 44. Head of the Weeping Woman.

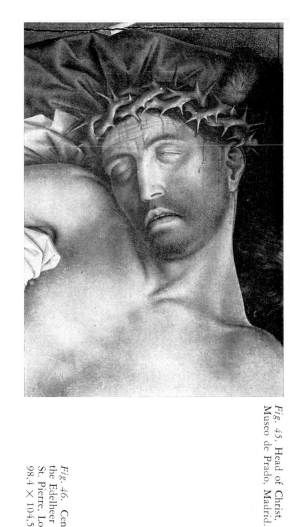

Fig. 45. Head of Christ, Museo de Prado, Madrid.

Fig. 47. Colijn de Coter, Descent from the Cross, Staatsgalerie, Stuttgart.

Fig. 46. Central panel of the Edelheer Triptych, St. Pierre, Louvain. 98,4 × 104,5 cm.

Fig. 48. Closed wings of the Edelheer Triptych.

Fig. 49. Mary Magdalen in the Braque Triptych, Musée du Louvre, Paris. 41 × 34,4 cm.

Fig. 50. Drawing of the Mary Magdalen, British Museum, London. 17,6 × 13 cm

Fig. 51. Mary and Christ in the Braque Triptych, *X-ray photograph.*

Fig. 52. Canon Henricus Werl with John the Baptist, Museo de Prado, Madrid. 101 × 47 cm.

Fig. 53. St. Barbara Reading, Museo de Prado, Madrid. 101 × 47 cm.

Fig. 55. Trinity, Hermitage, Leningrad. 28,5 × 18,5 cm.

Fig. 54. Virgin and Child, Hermitage, Leningrad. 28,5 × 18,5 cm.

Fig. 56. Trinity, Museum, Louvain. 124,5 × 90 cm.

Fig. 57. Colijn de Coter, Three Mourning Marys, Musée du Louvre, Paris.

Fig. 58. Virgin and Child in a Glory, Musée Granet, Aix-en-Provence. 48 × 31 cm.

Fig. 59. Virgin and Child, Staatliche Museen, Berlin-Dahlem. 38 × 26 cm.

Fig. 60. Betrothal of the Virgin, Museo de Prado, Madrid. 78 × 90 cm.

Fig. 61. St. James and St. Clara (reverse of the Betrothal), Museo de Prado, Madrid.

Figs. 62–63. Betrothal of the Virgin, *X-ray photographs.*

Fig. 65. Portrait of a Man, National Gallery, London, X-ray photograph.

Fig. 64. Portrait of a Man, National Gallery, London. 40,7 × 27 cm.

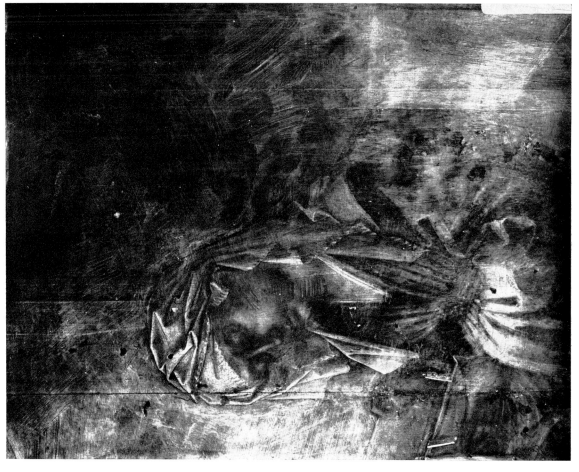

Fig. 66. Magdalen Reading, National Gallery, London. 61,5 × 54,5 cm.

Fig. 67. Magdalen Reading, National Gallery, London, X-ray photograph.

Fig. 69. Crucifixion, Musée Royal d'Art Ancien, Brussels, *X-ray photograph.*

Fig. 68. Crucifixion, Musée Royal d'Art Ancien, Brussels. 38 × 26,5 cm.

Fig. 70. Annunciation, Museo de Prado, Madrid. 70 × 76 cm.

Fig. 71. Annunciation, Musée Royal d'Art Ancien, Brussels. 58 × 64 cm.

Fig. 72. Virgin and Child with Saints, Kress Coll., National Gallery of Art, Washington. 119.4 × 148 cm.

Fig. 73. Detail at the bottom left, Kress Coll. National Gallery of Art, Washington.